25TH ANNIVERSARY:1974-1998

THE PLAYERS

CHAMPIONSHIP

®

American Golfer titles may be purchased for business or promotional use for special sales.
For information, please write to: Mr. Vince Laurentino, The American Golfer, Inc.,
151 Railroad Avenue, Greenwich, Connecticut 06830.

The AMERICAN GOLFER and its logo, its name in scripted letters, are trademarks of
The American Golfer, Inc.

FIRST EDITION

ISBN 1-888531-02-9

Published by:
The American Golfer, Inc.
151 Railroad Avenue
Greenwich, Connecticut 06830
(203) 862-9720
(203) 862-9724 FAX

Designed by:
NK Design
154 Parsons Drive
Hempstead, New York 11550
(516) 485-1610
(516) 485-1626 FAX

Film and Separations by:
Color Associates
10818 Midwest Ind. Blvd.
St. Louis, MO 63132
(314) 423-8080

ACKNOWLEDGMENTS
This book could not have been possible without the active assistance and editorial input of
John Morris and Henry Hughes of the PGA TOUR. Our sincerest thanks as well to John
Snow, Chuck Adams, Holly Carothers, Ana Leaird, Dave Lancer, Cathy Lewis and Ruth
Martin, also of the PGA TOUR.

Much appreciation to Don Wade for his writing skills.

Thanks also to Vince Laurentino and Juliet Zabik of The American Golfer.

Last, and certainly not least, thanks to our terrific art director, Nancy Koch of NK Design.

Photo Credits:
PGA TOUR: Jacket, Title Page, 6, 8-9, 10-11, 14-15, 24-25(inset), 26-27, 28-29, 30-31,
30-31(inset), 34-35, 34-35(inset), 36-37(inset), 38-39(inset), 40-41(inset), 42-43, 44-45,
46-47, 46-47(inset), 48-49, 50-51, 58-59, 58-59(inset), 60-61, 62-63(inset), 64-65, 66-67,
66-67(inset), 68-69, 70-71, 70-71(inset), 72-73, 74-75, 74-75(inset), 76-77, 78-79, 82-83,
82-83(inset), 84-85, 86-87, 86-87(inset), 90-91, 90-91(inset), 92-93, 94-95(inset), 96-97,
98-99, 98-99(inset), 100-101, 100-101(inset), 102-103, 102-103(inset), 104-105, 106-107,
106-107(inset), 108-109, 110-127; **ALLSPORT:** Table of Contents 88-89, 94-95; **Charles
R. Pugh:** 12-13; ***Golf World:*** 16-17, 18-19; ***Sports Illustrated:*** 20-21, 24-25 (John
Iacono); 32-33 (Walter Iooss, Jr.); 36-37 (Andy Hayt); 38-39, 52-53, 54-55(inset)
(Anthony Neste); 56-57; 62-63, 80-81 (Jacqueline Duvoisin); **The Associated Press:** 22-23;
AP/ World Wide Photos: 50-51(inset).

Artwork:
Bart Forbes: 108-109.

This book is dedicated to Deane R. Beman,
whose vision created THE PLAYERS Championship,
and to the thousands of volunteers who help the dream
come true every year.

25TH ANNIVERSARY: 1974-1998

THE PLAYERS
CHAMPIONSHIP
®

BY DON WADE AND MARTIN DAVIS

The American Golfer, Inc. ■ 151 Railroad Avenue ■ Greenwich, CT 06830 ■ tel. 203-862-9720 ■ fax: 203-862-9724

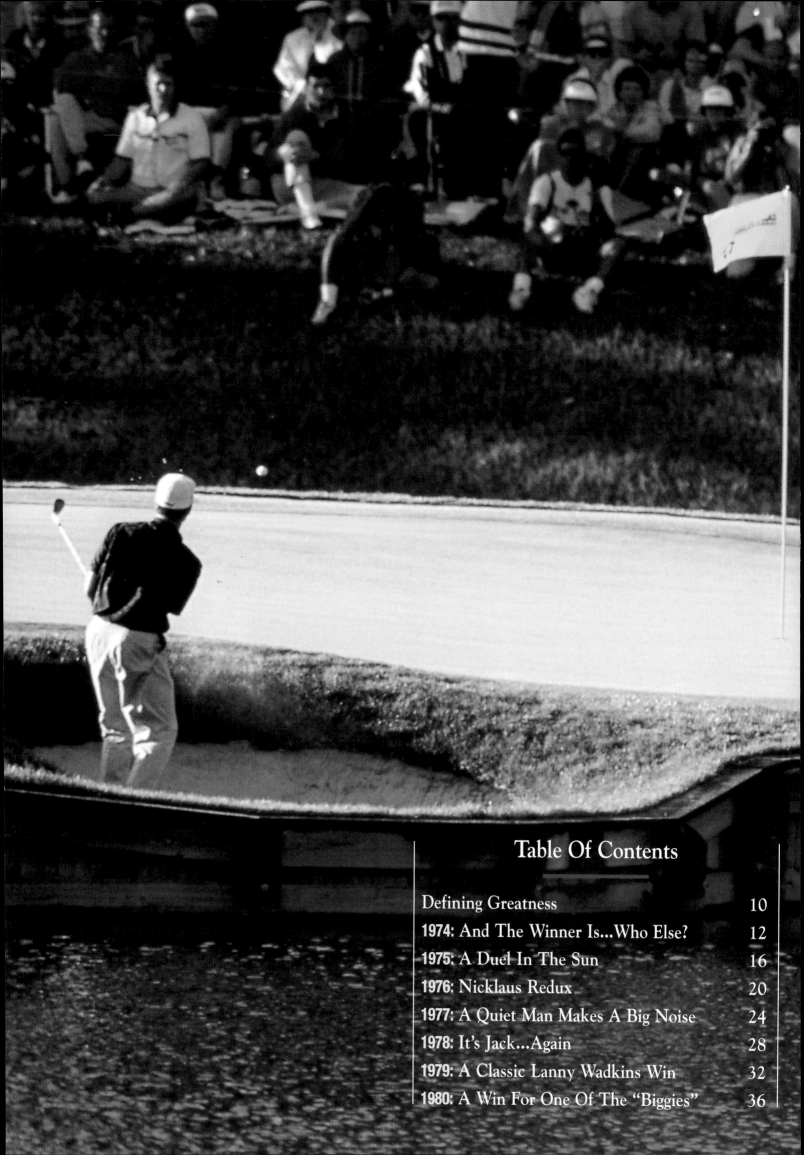

Table Of Contents

25TH ANNIVERSARY:1974-1998
THE PLAYERS
CHAMPIONSHIP

Defining Greatness

By Timothy W. Finchem, Commissioner PGA TOUR

Golf, golfers and golf events are defined in terms of greatness. As a singular endeavor, greatness in golf occurs if an individual is ready to seize the moment when the opportunity presents itself to raise his game and himself to another level.

Providing the best players in the world with that opportunity to excel was the reason THE PLAYERS Championship was created in 1974 and why the tournament is held in such high esteem by the players and the golfing public as it celebrates its Silver Anniversary in 1998.

Deane Beman, my predecessor as Commissioner of the PGA TOUR, had a vision for this event: bring the game's most outstanding players together to compete against each other in their own event on a supremely challenging test of golf.

Each year, the competitors in THE PLAYERS Championship offer valuable recommendations on how the course and the event itself can be improved. The Stadium Course at the Tournament Players Club at Sawgrass and the tournament operations are fine-tuned each year so the presentation of the event is as good as the strength of the field and the competition.

The best measure of the event's success is the stature of its champions. Nineteen of the previous 24 PLAYERS Champions also have won the Masters, the U.S. Open, the British Open or the PGA Championship.

Fittingly, Jack Nicklaus, who has a record 18 professional Majors to his credit, won when the event was first played (as the Tournament Players Championship) in 1974. Jack won again in 1976 and 1978 to become the tournament's only three-time champion. Fred Couples (1984, 1996) and Steve Elkington (1991, 1997) are the only two-time winners.

Winning THE PLAYERS Championship is no small feat. The event annually attracts the strongest field in golf from top to bottom. Just qualifying to play in the tournament is an accomplishment.

The best field in golf is tested over one of the game's outstanding championship layouts—the Stadium Course at the Tournament Players Club at Sawgrass, the site of the event since 1982. Designed by Pete Dye, the TPC at Sawgrass provides some of the most dramatic finishing holes in golf.

Few who were there will forget the eagle-by-inches by Fred Couples on the 16th hole when he stormed from four strokes behind to win the 1996 championship. And the famed island green of the 17th, the signature hole on the course, will test any player's courage under pressure.

The 18th, with the gallery lining the entire length of the hole, is one of the most beautiful - and difficult - final holes on any course. Steve Elkington put the finishing touches on an artistic winning performance in 1997 with a birdie at the home hole.

In these pages, you will be able to review year-by-year accounts of the event's great champions and great championships as well as a hole-by-hole description of the venue for this wonderful tournament.

The stadium Course is ready for the 25th chapter in the tournament's glorious history to be written. The 1998 PLAYERS Championship is another opportunity to define greatness.

1974

And The Winner Is...
Who Else?

So what if the rains came and the thunder cracked and play was delayed more than a few times? The first time it was played, THE PLAYERS Championship produced a supreme champion: Jack Nicklaus.

The first round at Atlanta Country Club saw J.C. Snead light up the course with a record-tying 64 at the same time heavy, intermittent rains were bogging down play. Thunderstorms caused three delays until play was finally suspended with 43 players still on the course. Nicklaus, one of those players, finished play the next morning with a 66.

Snead's second-round 71 left him a stroke behind Lou Graham, who shot a second 67 to take the lead. Snead continued to play well from tee to green, but the soft, wet greens caused him to leave putt after putt short of the hole. Nicklaus, with a 71, stayed close to the lead.

Snead looked like he might pull away from the field with a third-round 67 that gave him a total of 14-under-par 202 and a three-stroke lead over Nicklaus. With a national television audience looking on, Snead ended his round with a flourish. After hitting a good drive on the 509-yard, par-5 18th, he ripped a 4-wood second shot that easily carried the pond fronting the green, but came to rest in a shallow bunker behind the putting surface. He caught his bunker shot a bit thin, but the ball flew 30 feet into the hole for an eagle.

If he was looking over his shoulder at Nicklaus, he didn't let on.

"I don't care who's behind me," he said, sounding an awful lot like his legendary uncle, Sam. "When I'm playing good, I believe I can beat anyone in golf."

The final round turned into a Sunday/Monday overnight affair as thunderstorms again rolled through Georgia.

Snead expanded his lead to five strokes early Sunday when he had birdies on the first two holes to Nicklaus' pars, but that lead wouldn't last for long. Snead missed the green

1974

on the third hole and made a bogey. When Nicklaus birdied the hole, the lead was cut to three strokes. A few minutes and a Nicklaus birdie on No. 4 later, and the lead was cut to two.

An Arnold Palmer charge might be electric, but Jack Nicklaus in his prime, closing in on the lead, was absolutely relentless.

On the sixth hole, Snead drew a bad lie in a bunker and bogeyed. Nicklaus birdied and caught Snead for the first time. Five holes later, facing the round's third rain delay, Nicklaus's group was invited into a couple's nearby house for a snack and a little television. Refreshed, Jack immediately made a birdie that gave him the lead. He never looked back.

Nicklaus pushed his lead to two strokes with a birdie on the short, par-3 13th when he hit a wedge to eight feet and made the putt—moments before a storm forced another delay. Shortly afterwards, play was suspended for the day.

If Snead spent a restless night, it's certainly understandable. Not only did he have time to mull over what he'd been through, but he almost certainly knew what was coming when play resumed.

On Monday, Nicklaus picked up where he left off, with a 23-foot birdie putt on 14 that got him to 17-under-par and three strokes clear of Snead. A bogey on the par-3 16th only hurt him in style points.

The tournament was all but over.

THE PLAYERS Championship had just the kind of inaugural winner it needed.

A tradition had been born.

TOP PLAYERS OF 1974

WINNER:			
JACK NICKLAUS		66-71-68-67—272	$ 50,000.
J.C. SNEAD	2	64-71-67-72—274	$ 28,500.
BRUCE CRAMPTON	3	69-68-72-67—276	$ 17,750.
GENE LITTLER	4	72-69-69-67—277	$ 11,750.
LOU GRAHAM	5	67-67-73-71—278	$ 10,250.
BOB MURPHY	T6	71-71-69-68—279	$ 8,500.
HUBERT GREEN	T6	70-67-72-70—279	$ 8,500.
DAVE HILL	8	70-66-72-72—280	$ 7,375.
CHARLES COODY	T9	67-71-71-72—281	$ 6,250.
BUDDY ALLIN	T9	71-67-71-72—281	$ 6,250.
EDDIE PIERCE	T9	73-67-69-72—281	$ 6,250.

1975

A Duel In The Sun

When the 1975 PLAYERS Championship came to Fort Worth's celebrated Colonial Country Club in August, everyone expected heat; but few people predicted how hot Al Geiberger would be that week.

The 1966 PGA Champion, Geiberger had played well in 1975 after enduring a long and frustrating slump. He had played beautifully at Colonial in pre-tournament rounds and, when he opened with a 66 in the blistering 100-plus degree heat, it gave an obvious boost to his confidence—especially since he did a lot of his damage on the greens, where he one-putted 11 times. Defending champion Jack Nicklaus, Bob Dickson and Hale Irwin were a stroke back.

Geiberger added a second-round 68 for a two-stroke lead over his good friend and fellow USC alumnus Dave Stockton, whose 64 was highlighted by a record-breaking 30 on the front side. A heavy thunderstorm raked the course in the afternoon, breaking the heat but stranding 34 players who had to finish their rounds Saturday morning.

Geiberger extended his lead over Stockton to three strokes after a third-round 67, but it was a far from easy 67. On the front nine, Geiberger missed five greens, hit two balls into the water, put one in a bunker and still shot an even-par 35. The score gave Geiberger a 54-hole total of 201, a Colonial record.

Stockton, who won at Colonial in 1967, predicted his good friend would be difficult to catch. "This is a good course to protect a lead," he explained. "As long as you shoot a good final round, nobody can come out of the pack and gun you down."

Maybe, but Stockton sure tried.

Both players came out and shot 69s on a day which saw Geiberger extend his lead to four strokes at one point while Stockton actually held the lead twice.

Playing ahead of Geiberger, Stockton struck first with a birdie on the first hole, but the leader matched him a few minutes later.

1975

Geiberger stretched his lead to four strokes with a birdie on the par-4 third, but the tournament soon tightened.

Geiberger hit both his drive and approach into the rough on the fifth hole and made a bogey while, up ahead, Stockton was sinking a 15-foot birdie putt on the sixth green.

With his lead cut to two strokes, Geiberger stumbled again on No. 7 when he three-putted from the back edge. When Geiberger bogeyed the eighth hole, he and Stockton were tied.

Stockton took the lead for the first time with a birdie on the difficult ninth hole. Geiberger settled himself and birdied 11 to catch Stockton, only to fall behind again with a bogey on the next hole when he drove the ball into the thick rough. Geiberger righted himself with a birdie on 13 when he hit a 3-iron to 12 feet and made the putt to draw even with Stockton again.

"That was the birdie I really needed," Geiberger said. "It restored my confidence."

Geiberger regained the lead for good when Stockton bogeyed the 14th, and all but locked up the tournament when he birdied the 15th while Stockton, a superb putter, uncharacteristically three-putted the 16th.

"If anybody had told me I'd finish at 7-under and not win, I wouldn't have believed them," Stockton said. "I threw everything I had at Allen. There are very few people who could play as well as he did under the pressure."

Geiberger, who led from wire-to-wire and shot four rounds in the 60s to set a Colonial record, modestly agreed.

"When you're leading all week, there's no pressure like it," he said.

Or thrill like it, either.

TOP PLAYERS OF 1975

WINNER: AL GEIBERGEER		66-68-67-69—270	$ 50,000.
DAVE STOCKTON	2	72-64-68-69—273	$ 28,500.
HUBERT GREEN	3	71-65-70-69—275	$ 17,730.
BOB MURPHY	T4	73-69-71-68—281	$ 10,333.
BOB DICKSON	T4	67-69-72-73—281	$ 10,333.
MASON RUDOLPH	T4	69-70-72-70—281	$ 10,333.
HALE IRWIN	7	67-72-72-72—283	$ 8,000.
TOM WATSON	T8	73-69-75-67—284	$ 6,791.
JOE PORTER	T8	72-72-68-72—284	$ 6,791.
BOBBY WADKINS	T8	76-69-68-71—284	$ 6,791.

Joseph C. Dey, Jr.
Trophy

THE PROFESSIONAL GOLFERS' ASSOCIATION OF AME

1976

Nicklaus Redux

Winning a golf tournament is rarely easy, but it's especially difficult in bad weather. But, if patience is a virtue—then Jack Nicklaus is a very virtuous man.

The 1976 PLAYERS Championship was plagued by rains that led to numerous delays and made the course slow and soft, just the opposite of the hard and fast championship conditions Nicklaus prefers. Still, by the end of tournament, Nicklaus had stoically waited out the conditions and out-played the field—just as he has done so many times.

The tournament was played at Inverrary Golf and Country Club in south Florida, and, for a time, the weather threatened to make the place look more like the Everglades than a golf course. Downpours drenched the course on Wednesday, and Thursday's first round was delayed for more than an hour by morning rains. After a brief respite, the rains resumed in the afternoon and, combined with the gathering darkness, forced a postponement with 33 players on the course. One of them was Nicklaus, who was 5-under-par after 16 holes, and trailed the leader, Fred Marti, by a stroke. Marti's 66 also was a stroke ahead of Tom Watson, J.C. Snead and Don January, who had finished their rounds.

The leader after two rounds was Don January, who shot a 68 to put him in at 9-under-par 135, which surprised many people. It's not that January wasn't a fine player. Indeed, the 1967 PGA Champion had won 11 times on TOUR. But he was 46 years old and had just returned from two and a half years off the TOUR while he built and designed golf courses. Two shots behind January were Nicklaus and Snead.

Saturday's third round was totally washed out and rescheduled for Sunday. It quickly developed into a duel between Nicklaus and Snead, who both shot 68s to tie for the lead at 12-under-par. January shot a 73 to fall three strokes off the race. A stroke behind the leaders were Mark Hayes (67) and Roger Maltbie (65). The final round

1976

1976 promised to be a replay of the inaugural tournament two years earlier, when Nicklaus edged Snead by two strokes at Atlanta C.C.

This time Jack got J.C. by three—but it took some inspired play to do it.

Snead shot a 68 for a total of 272, which bettered the previous four-round course record. Not that it did him much good.

Both players birdied the par-5 second hole, but then Nicklaus took off. He hit a 1-iron to five feet for a birdie on the fifth hole, then reached the 578-yard, par-5 eighth hole in two and made another birdie. Nicklaus added birdies on the 12th and 13th holes; but, to his credit, so did Snead, who was hitting the ball close to the hole all day but not making any putts.

Nicklaus had to scramble a bit on the last two holes. His drive on 17 flirted with the water but stayed dry. His 7-iron approach came to rest in the back fringe, but he chipped to within three feet and saved par. On 18, he pushed his 3-wood into the right rough behind a stand of trees. His 8-iron second shot cleared the trees but left him short of the green. His pitch stopped six feet from the hole and he made the putt after watching Snead hole a 60-foot bunker shot for a birdie.

In the end, a frustrated but respectful Snead summed up the feelings of many fellow PGA TOUR members when it came to playing against Jack Nicklaus.

"What am I supposed to do, say he's God and everybody else should stay home?" Snead said. "I didn't quit, but what could you do?"

Good question.

TOP PLAYERS OF 1976

WINNER:			
JACK NICKLAUS		66-70-68-65—269	$ 60,000.
J.C. SNEAD	2	67-69-68-68—272	$ 34,200.
JIM MASSERIO	T3	69-68-72-67—276	$ 17,700.
ROGER MALTBIE	T3	70-70-65-71—276	$ 17,700.
MARK HAYES	5	71-67-67-72—277	$ 12,300.
LEE ELDER	6	69-72-70-67—278	$ 10,800.
DON JANUARY	T7	67-68-73-72—280	$ 9,225.
BUTCH BAIRD	T7	71-67-72-70—280	$ 9,225.
GARY PLAYER	T9	73-70-71-67—281	$ 7,500.
DAVID GRAHAM	T9	70-71-71-69—281	$ 7,500.
TOM WATSON	T9	67-70-70-74—281	$ 7,500.

1977

A Quiet Man Makes A Big Noise

Every once in a while, a golf tournament takes on a fairy tale quality. That was certainly the case at the 1977 PLAYERS Championship. The championship had moved to Sawgrass Country Club, a demanding course in Ponte Vedra Beach, FL that had been re-designed by PGA TOUR veteran Gardner Dickinson and promised difficult scoring—to say the least.

But the first round saw Mike McCullough—an unlikely leader by his own admission—shoot a course-record 66, a six-under-par score that gave him a two-stroke lead over Raymond Floyd, Tom Watson and Don Bies. McCullough had just a tie for fourth to show as his best finish in his first four years on TOUR.

Winds gusted to 40 miles per-hour to send scores soaring for the second round. The average score was 77, pushing the cut to a tournament-record 11-over-par 155. Given all that, McCullough could have been excused if he'd shot himself out of the tournament, but he hung tough and shot a 74 for a 140 total that left him with a two-stroke lead over Tom Watson.

"I was very pleased with the 74," McCullough said, pointing out that just two players had broken par with 71s. "If I had shot a 66 today, you'd have to give me a saliva test."

Sneaking quietly up the leader board with a second-round 74 of his own was 27-year old Mark Hayes, who had won twice in his three and a half years on TOUR.

When, in the relative calm of Saturday's third round, Hayes shot a 71, he suddenly found himself a stroke out of the even-par lead shared by the persistent McCullough and the tenacious Watson.

"I sort of feel like a rabbit with wolves all around," said McCullough, who was realistic, if not necessarily confident, about his chances.

Still, after three rounds, McCullough clung to a piece of the lead.

1977

The big names near the top of the leader board fell away early on Sunday. Hale Irwin, whose 69 on Saturday had moved him into contention, bogeyed all four par-5s and had to settle for a 74 and a tie for third. Had he made four pars, he would have won the tournament. Watson, another notoriously tough competitor, had a miserable back nine with four bogeys in five holes, beginning on No. 11. He shot a 77 and finished five strokes out of the lead.

With all the wreckage piling up around him, Hayes went about his business like the Stealth Golfer. After a bogey on the par-3 third hole, he got back to even par for the round with a birdie on 14, only to give it back with a bogey on 17 where he failed to get up and down from a bunker.

McCullough managed just two birdies on the day against three bogeys and a double-bogey, but was just a stroke off the lead as Hayes came to the final hole. For a time, it looked as though a playoff was inevitable.

Hayes flew his second shot on the par-5 finishing hole into a bunker behind the green. The ball was on a downslope, leaving Hayes an extremely difficult shot under the best of conditions—let alone on the final hole of THE PLAYERS Championship.

But Hayes kept his cool and played a remarkable shot. He chose a 5-iron, pitched the ball over the sand and safely onto the green, where it rolled smoothly to within 10 feet of the hole. With a one-stroke lead, Hayes might have been expected to two-putt for the win. Instead, he holed the putt for a dramatic two-stroke victory.

And a fairy tale ending of his own.

TOP PLAYERS OF 1977

WINNER:			
MARK HAYES		72-74-71-72—289	$ 60,000.
MIKE McCULLOUGH	2	66-74-76-75—291	$ 34,200.
BRUCE DEVLIN	T3	69-79-72-72—292	$ 17,700.
HALE IRWIN	T3	72-77-69-74—292	$ 17,700.
GRAHAM MARSH	T5	73-77-72-71—293	$ 10,900.
JACK NICKLAUS	T5	73-74-72-74—293	$ 10,900.
TOM WATSON	T5	68-74-74-77—293	$ 10,900.
BILL ROGERS	T8	75-72-76-71—294	$ 8,150.
STEVE MELNYK	T8	73-76-73-72—294	$ 8,150.
LARRY NELSON	T8	74-74-73-73—294	$ 8,150.

1978

It's Jack...Again

Jack Nicklaus had three things going for him coming into the 1978 PLAYERS Championship.

■ He had won the championship two of the previous four times it had been played.

■ Of the four tournaments he had played that spring, he had won once and finished second twice.

■ And he was Jack Nicklaus.

Nicklaus opened with a two-under par 70 that left him in a seven-way tie for the lead. But he served notice to the rest of the field when he made four birdies in a five-hole stretch on the incoming nine.

When the players arrived at Sawgrass Country Club, near the ocean, for the second round, they faced a pair of 35s—35-mile-per-hour winds combined with a 35-degree temperature. While the weather would improve as the day wore on, par would remain a treasured score for the round. Nicklaus shot a 71 to share the lead with Ben Crenshaw and 1975 U.S. Open Champion Lou Graham. The cut, at nine-over-par 153, was the championship's second highest to date.

Nicklaus got off to a Jack-like start in the third round with birdies on the first two holes and a par on the par-3 third. Then, inexplicably, he hit his second shot into the water on the par-5 fourth hole for a double bogey.

"Just the way I planned it," Nicklaus said. "A start of 3-3-3-7."

Nicklaus finished with a 73 for a 214 total which left him a stroke ahead of Graham, who had stumbled to a 40 on the outward nine, but recovered to shoot a 74 for 215. They were the only players under par after 54 holes.

One other point of interest from Saturday's third round was Mike McCullough's 69. Added to his first two rounds of 77 and 75, this left him at 221, seven-strokes behind Nicklaus. Why mention it then? Because it was the only sub-70 round to that point in the tournament—and there wouldn't be another one.

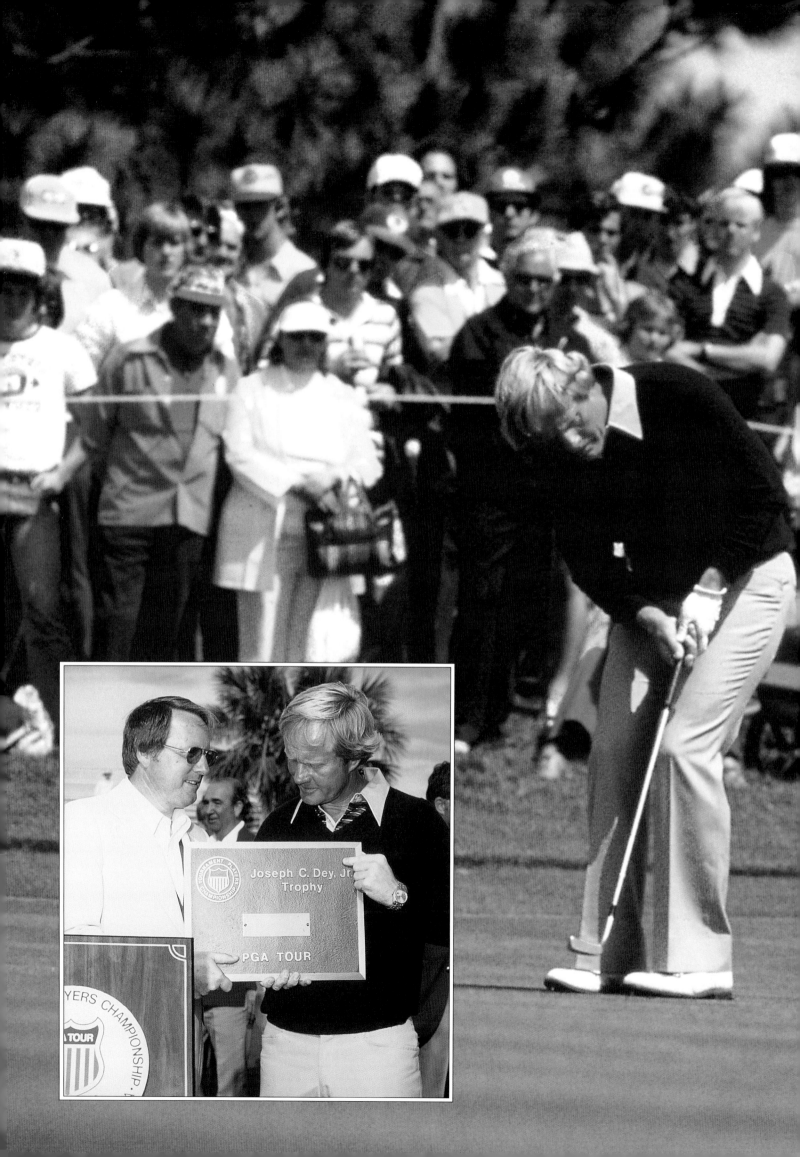

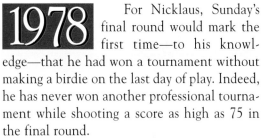

1978

For Nicklaus, Sunday's final round would mark the first time—to his knowledge—that he had won a tournament without making a birdie on the last day of play. Indeed, he has never won another professional tournament while shooting a score as high as 75 in the final round.

All that's not to say there weren't moments of excitement.

Graham, playing ahead of Nicklaus, bogeyed the first and ninth holes, then birded the 11th by knocking a sand shot to within a foot of the hole. When Nicklaus three-putted 12, the two were briefly tied for the lead at even par.

Graham fell out of the lead with bogeys on the 14th and 16th holes when he failed to get up and down from bunkers. Nicklaus dropped a shot on 17, only his second bogey on the inward nine, which left him with a thin, one-stroke lead going to 18.

Nicklaus, guarding against a water hazard to the left side of the landing area, blocked his drive to the right. The ball came to rest behind a palm tree, which prevented Nicklaus from making a full swing. Nicklaus chose a 3-iron and struck the ball just before the club's shaft hit the tree. The ball ran across the fairway and into the left rough 160 yards from the hole. Nicklaus hit a 7-iron 45 feet from the pin, ran his approach putt to within three feet and made the putt for his 65th TOUR victory.

"I didn't win this tournament," Nicklaus said later. "I was just the only one to survive."

TOP PLAYERS OF 1978

WINNER:			
JACK NICKLAUS		70-71-73-75—289	$ 60,000.
LOU GRAHAM	2	71-70-74-75—290	$ 34,200.
LON HINKLE	3	75-72-74-70—291	$ 21,300.
JOHN SCHROEDER	T4	70-75-76-71—292	$ 11,700.
BEN CRENSHAW	T4	70-71-77-74—292	$ 11,700.
LARRY NELSON	T4	71-72-75-74—292	$ 11,700.
ANDY NORTH	T4	74-71-74-73—292	$ 11,700.
JIM COLBERT	8	74-74-74-72—294	$ 8,850.
HUBERT GREEN	T9	76-77-71-71—295	$ 7,500.
VICTOR REGALADO	T9	70-79-76-70—295	$ 7,500.
PETER OOSTERHUIS	T9	73-73-75-74—295	$ 7,500.

1979

A Classic
Lanny Wadkins Win

In the long history of golf, there have been few players as ready to face down a challenge as Lanny Wadkins. Aggressive by nature, he has always excelled under difficult, pressure-packed conditions.

That made him the perfect man for the 1979 PLAYERS Championship.

The event at Sawgrass Country Club began under remarkably benign conditions for a tournament played on a course near the ocean in March. Kermit Zarley tied the course record with a 66 on a day that saw 53 players break par while 21 others shot even-par 72s. A stroke behind Zarley were Jack Nicklaus, Andy North and Wadkins, who sized up the conditions and "hit it at the flag all day."

The conditions stayed calm through Friday morning, and George Burns took advantage by shooting a 66 of his own to finish at 138. Wadkins, playing in wind and rain in the afternoon, shot a remarkable 68 to take a three-stroke over Burns. It was, Wadkins admitted, "one of the finest rounds I've ever played." Gary Player called it "an absolutely unbelievable score."

Then, the weather worsened. People who watched, let alone played in, Saturday's third round still shake their heads in amazement. The conditions bordered on unplayable, with 40-mile-per-hour winds tearing across the course, and occasionally gusting even higher. How bad was it?

Item: the average score was 77.5.

Item: Fourteen players shot 80 or higher, including Jack Nicklaus, who had 10 pars and a birdie and still shot an 82.

Item: Jack Renner's one-under par 71 was the low score for the day.

Wadkins shot a 76 that gave him a a three-round total of five-under-par 211, good enough for a three-stroke lead over Renner, Burns, Lee Trevino and Bill Kratzert. Burns, who had known Wadkins since their amateur days, didn't think anyone would catch the leader.

"Lanny is aggressive and he's a winner," Burns

1979 said. "He won't back off. Anyone who wins will have to take it away from him."

No one was taking anything away from Lanny Wadkins this time around.

If possible, conditions were even more brutal on Sunday. The winds rose to 45 miles per hour and the average score ballooned to 78.5. Wadkins had an up-and-down—but remarkable—round. He bogeyed the first hole, but came back with a birdie on No. 2 when he sank a 40-foot putt. His biggest scare came minutes later when Kratzert, playing in the group ahead of Wadkins, birdied two of the first four holes to cut Wadkins' lead to a single stroke. But it was a short-lived challenge as Kratzert went four-over for the last five holes of the outward nine and finished with a 79.

Tom Watson was the only other player to make a run at Wadkins. The TOUR's leading money winner in 1977 and 1978, Watson birdied the par-3 12th hole and, when Wadkins bogeyed the hole minutes later, the lead was cut to three strokes. But Watson fell back with a bogey on 15 and Wadkins was able to put it on cruise control. He parred 16 then holed a difficult putt to save par on 17.

Anyone who had followed Wadkins' career could see he was like a horse struggling against the reins. Playing for pars might be the smart way to protect a lead, but Lanny Wadkins didn't get to be Lanny Wadkins by playing for pars.

On 18, with the strong crosswinds blowing towards a water hazard, he lashed a drive into the fairway then hit a bold second shot on the par 5. He came up short of the green, but chipped to 12 feet and finished true to form—with a birdie that gave him the day's only under-par round.

It was a classic Lanny Wadkins performance—one people still talk about to this day.

Top Players of 1979			
Winner: **Lanny Wadkins**		67-68-76-72—283	$ 72,000.
Tom Watson	2	70-72-75-71—288	$ 43,200.
Jack Renner	3	73-70-71-75—289	$ 27,200.
Phil Hancock	4	69-73-75-74—291	$ 19,200.
Wayne Levi	T5	69-72-77-75—293	$ 14,600.
Bill Kratzert	T5	69-70-75-79—293	$ 14,600.
Lee Trevino	T5	70-69-75-79—293	$ 14,600.
Andy Bean	8	72-73-74-75—294	$ 12,400.
Tom Kite	T9	72-73-75-75—295	$ 10,800.
Jack Newton, Jr.	T9	69-74-77-75—295	$ 10,800.

THE PLAYERS
CHAMPIONSHIP

1980

A Win For One Of
The "Biggies"

L ee Trevino long has had a theory about what
makes a great golf tournament. "The tougher
the golf courses are," Trevino explains,
"That's when you get the biggest names on
the leader board."

If that's the case, Sawgrass, the site of the
1980 PLAYERS Championship, must have been
a killer that year. By the last round, it was "All-
Star Golf" time in Ponte Vedra Beach, Fla.

The first round began quietly enough,
under relatively calm conditions for the seaside
course, which is characteristically buffeted by
strong winds in March. Former U.S. and
British Amateur Champion Steve Melnyk and
two-time U.S. Open Champion Hale Irwin
tied for the lead with 5-under-par 67s. In all,
53 players broke par.

"Sawgrass played as easy as we'll ever find it,"
said Jack Nicklaus, who hit 16 green in regulation
en route to a 69. "We'll get wind before the week
is out."

On Friday, winds gusted to 40 miles per
hour, play was suspended for an hour by a thunderstorm, and the game was on. Irwin shot a par
72 to share the lead at 5-under-par 139 with
Curtis Strange who shot a 71. A stroke back
were Trevino, Melnyk and Tom Watson.

Trevino made his move on Saturday, shooting a 68 in the calm, sunny conditions. His round
was highlighted by playing the four par-5s in 3-
under par—a testimonial to his remarkable skill
from 100 yards in. Hubert Green was a stroke
back but on Sunday, all eyes would be on the
final group—Trevino, Nicklaus and Gary Player.

Nicklaus and Player got off to a fast start, each
making birdie on the first hole. Trevino bogeyed
the second hole, but used it as a wake-up call.

"I'll admit it made me mad," Trevino said.
"Those guys are coming at me early, and I help
them by throwing one away on two."

Trevino reacted by making birdies on the
fourth and fifth holes, then followed with two
more birdies on the ninth and 10th, to get to 10

25th Anniversary
37

THE PLAYERS
CHAMPIONSHIP

1980

under par and take a three-stroke lead.

But playing ahead of Trevino was Ben Crenshaw, who was blistering the course with birdies on the second, eighth, ninth and 10th holes. After birdies on the 15th and 17th, Crenshaw was one stroke behind Trevino with the par-5 18th left to play.

Trevino birdied 15 to get his lead back to two strokes, but bogeyed 16 when he put his approach shot into a bunker, hit his third shot long, then missed coming back, leaving himself a dangerous three-footer for bogey that trickled into the hole.

Ahead on 18, Crenshaw, easily one of the game's greatest putters, stood over a downhill 15-footer for birdie. The ball rolled steadily towards the center of the cup, but as the gallery's roar swelled, the ball veered to the left at the last moment.

Par. And a two-stroke lead for Trevino.

Trevino walked quickly to the 18th tee and drove the ball safely in the fairway. He pulled a 6-iron and laid up just under 100 yards out.

"I hit it right where I wanted it," Trevino said.

Right where he could take a full swing with his wedge and send the ball in low and spinning. The ball landed, bounced briefly, then checked up sharply just 15-feet from the hole. Two careful putts later, Trevino was home free.

Later, a writer asked Trevino if he'd felt intimidated being paired with Nicklaus and Player.

"Hell no," he said. "I'm one of the biggies, too."

TOP PLAYERS OF 1980

WINNER: LEE TREVINO		68-72-68-70—278	$ 72,000.
BEN CRENSHAW	2	71-73-69-66—279	$ 28,500.
SEVE BALLESTEROS	T3	69-73-69-69—280	$ 23,200.
TOM WATSON	T3	69-71-72-68—280	$ 23,200.
MIKE REID	T5	70-72-72-68—282	$ 14,600.
JOHN MAHAFFEY	T5	70-71-72-69—282	$ 14,600.
PETER JACOBSEN	T5	68-74-69-71—282	$ 14,600.
GRIER JONES	T8	74-69-72-68—283	$ 10,400.
DAN POHL	T8	73-72-69-69—283	$ 10,400.
DANNY EDWARDS	T8	68-74-72-69—283	$ 10,400.
JAY HAAS	T8	72-73-67-71—283	$ 10,400.
HUBERT GREEN	T8	72-71-66-74—283	$ 10,400.
GARY PLAYER	T8	70-71-69-73—283	$ 10,400.

1981

A Tough Man
For A Tough Job

Midway through the 1981 PLAYERS Championship, veteran John Mahaffey took a look at the playing conditions and made a most astute observation.

"The guy who wins will be the one with the most patience and best short game," Mahaffey predicted. "You can't go for a lot of pins on this course, in these conditions. You've got to shoot for par, which is a good score. This golf course will take its toll from the guys who don't play it smart."

Anyone who followed golf knew one player he was describing perfectly: the eventual champion, Raymond Floyd.

Sawgrass was playing host to the tournament for the fifth and last time and proved early that it wasn't letting go without a struggle. Brutal 30-mile-per-hour winds greeted the field in the first round and, by the time play finished on the seaside course, players were literally reeling from the experience.

Of the 144 players, only 13 managed to break par, led by Mike Morley, who had won just once on TOUR, and three-time TOUR winner Dave Eichelberger. The average score on the par-72 course was a whopping 75.63, and 20 players shot 80 or higher.

The second round proved to be much the same. The March winds continued to pummel players, and it was left to one-time TOUR winner Barry Jaeckel to take the lead with a 2-under par 70 which left him in with a 5-under-par 139. One back were Danny Edwards and Canada's Dan Halldorson. After a 68, Jack Nicklaus was four back and considered himself lucky to be that close.

"There were a few shots out there I didn't know how to play," said the three-time winner of the championship. "At Augusta, you want to get the ball up the air. Here, if you do that, you'll have to go find it. I actually like this course. I just don't like playing it in a gale."

Floyd, for his part, shot rounds of 72-74—

1981

146, but no one was counting him out, especially in difficult conditions. Nor were they counting out Curtis Strange, whose back-to-back 72s made him another candidate to fulfill Mahaffey's prediction.

Jaeckel went out and shot a gutsy 72 in the third round to widen his lead to three strokes, but even he admitted that the pressure and the conditions were starting to take their toll.

"I don't mind telling you my swing started going to the dogs in the last six holes," he said. "I was tired, my nerves were frayed, I could feel a little choke setting in, and I wanted to get the hell in as soon as possible."

All that, and one round still to go.

To his great credit, Jaeckel hung tough in the final round of the biggest tournament of his life, shooting a 74 which got him into a playoff with two of the TOUR's most respected competitors, Floyd and Strange.

Watching the leaderboards could not have been pleasant for Jaeckel, as Floyd relentlessly moved in with birdies on the sixth, 11th, 12th and 15th holes. Strange shot a 70 to tie Floyd, who was first to finish, then both men watched as Jaeckel left a seven-foot birdie putt short of the hole on 18.

The playoff began and ended on the 175-yard, par-3 15th. All three players missed the green with their 6-iron tee shots. Floyd, with the best lie, chipped to within a foot for a tap-in par. Strange chipped to eight feet and missed. Jaeckel's chip finished five feet from the hole, but he missed and Floyd had won the 14th of his 22 TOUR titles.

"I didn't lose the tournament," Jaeckel said. "I was beaten by a great player."

No one could disagree.

TOP PLAYERS OF 1981

WINNER:			
RAYMOND FLOYD		72-74-71-68—285	$ 72,000.
CURTIS STRANGE	T2	72-72-71-70—285	$ 35,200.
BARRY JAECKEL	T2	69-70-72-74—285	$ 35,200.
MILLER BARBER	T4	72-78-69-68—287	$ 15,750.
JIM COLBERT	T4	78-69-69-71—287	$ 15,750.
BRUCE LIETZKE	T4	73-75-68-71—287	$ 15,750.
JIM SIMONS	T4	73-68-73-73—287	$ 15,750.
LEONARD THOMPSON	T8	71-76-72-69—288	$ 11,200.
GARY HALLBERG	T8	71-73-72-72—288	$ 11,200.
FRANK CONNER	T8	74-72-70-72—288	$ 11,200.
DAN HALLDORSON	T8	70-70-74-74—288	$ 11,200.

1982

Pate Makes His Big Splash

When a tournament moves to a brand new course, officials naturally hope that the winner is a player of impeccable pedigree. No flukes need apply. And if he has a bit of the showman in him, so much the better.

All of which made Jerry Pate a dream come true when THE PLAYERS Championship came to its new home, the Stadium Course at the Tournament Players Club at Sawgrass in 1982. Pate was one of the TOUR's marquee players. The 1974 U.S. Amateur champion had turned pro in 1975 and made his first victory a good one—the 1976 U.S. Open.

Naturally Pate, with his long, flowing swing and flair for the dramatic, was one of the pre-tournament favorites. But he struggled on the greens in the first round, taking 30 putts en route to a 70 which left him three strokes behind leaders Larry Nelson, Lyn Lott and George Burns. In all, 56 players shot par or better, with 17 scoring in the 60s.

"I would have been concerned if somebody hadn't shot a 67," said course architect Pete Dye. "The conditions were good enough and certainly the players are good enough to post that kind of number on any course."

The field bunched together in the second round, with Hale Irwin, Scott Simpson, Vance Heafner, Tim Simpson and Lott sharing the lead at 6-under par 138. There was an impressive list of players within striking distance, including Pate, Craig Stadler, Tom Kite, Bruce Lietzke, Bill Rogers and Seve Ballesteros.

As is so often the case, Saturday's third round completely scrambled the leaderboard. Irwin and Tim Simpson fell back with uncharacteristic 75s and were three strokes out of the lead. Haas and Lott fell even further back. Bruce Lietzke's 69 vaulted him into a tie for the lead with Brad Bryant. But those who closely checked the day's statistics knew that one player to watch was Lietzke's brother-in-law, Jerry Pate, who shot a 70 while taking just 26 putts—eight fewer than the day before—and was three strokes back.

To no one's surprise, Lietzke started quickly on Sunday. He birdied the first two holes—and after seven holes—had a two-stroke lead over Bryant,

1982

led Pate by four and looked unbeatable.

Then the new course struck back. Lietzke bogeyed the eighth and ninth holes to fall into a tie with Bryant. When Pate birdied No. 12 and Bryant bogeyed the 11th, Lietzke had a one-stroke lead. But when Pate and Bryant both birdied 14, there was a three-way tie at the top.

Pate, playing ahead of Lietzke and Bryant, failed to birdie the 16th. On 17, he hit an 8-iron to 15 feet. Moments later, he watched Lietzke hit his 2-iron approach in the water on 16. When Pate birdied and Lietzke bogeyed, there was a dramatic two-shot swing.

But Bryant was still very much around after a birdie on 16 that put him one behind Pate. Also alive was Scott Simpson, who birdied the final three holes to tie Bryant.

Despite the tremendous pressure, Pate laced a drive down the left side of the 18th fairway, flirting briefly with the water. Then, in an eerie repetition of the 5-iron he knocked stiff on the 72nd hole to lock up the 1976 U.S. Open, Pate again pulled his 5-iron and took aim at the flag. The ball tore off the clubface and rose against the clear blue sky. It landed softly and came to rest 18 inches from the hole to insure his victory. Remarkably, his eight-under par 280 was precisely the winning score predicted by Dye at the start of the championship.

All in all, it was a successful baptism for the new course. Still, Pate had one last trick up his sleeve. With a huge gallery and a national television audience looking on, he tossed the course's designer, Pete Dye, and the TOUR's Commissioner, Deane Beman, into the greenside lake—and then, with a theatrical flourish, dove in himself.

Top Players of 1982

WINNER:			
JERRY PATE		70-73-70-67—280	$ 90,000.
SCOTT SIMPSON	T2	72-64-68-69—273	$ 44,000.
BRAD BRYANT	T2	70-69-71-72—282	$ 44,000.
BRUCE LIETZKE	4	69-72-69-73—283	$ 24,000.
ROGER MALTBIE	5	69-72-73-70—284	$ 20,000.
HUBERT GREEN	T6	73-75-70-68—286	$ 16,187.
CRAIG STADLER	T6	71-68-75-72—286	$ 16,187.
TOM WATSON	T6	70-76-68-72—286	$ 16,187.
SEVE BALLESTEROS	T6	73-72-69-72—286	$ 16,187.
JIM BOOROS	T10	73-72-71-71—287	$ 12,500.
LARRY NELSON	T10	67-72-77-71—287	$ 12,500.
ED SNEED	T10	68-71-74-74—287	$ 12,500.

1983

It's Sutton, In
A Sunday Shoot-Out

From the moment they won their respective U.S. Amateur Championships, people had expected big things from Hal Sutton and John Cook, the 1983 PLAYERS Championship proved that those expectations were well founded. In the end, it came down to a wild final round that saw Sutton, the 1980 Amateur champion, edge Cook, who had won the Amateur in 1978, by a stroke.

The 10th PLAYERS Championship began on a soggy note as heavy rains soaked the Stadium Course at the Tournament Players Club at Sawgrass, forcing the postponement of the first round until Friday. When play got underway, Bruce Lietzke shot a four-under-par 68 in calm conditions to take a one-stroke lead over Cook, Mark McCumber and Leonard Thompson.

Cook, a stylish shot-maker who was fighting an arm injury he suffered a year earlier, surged to a two-stroke lead with a 70 in the breezy-but-dry second round. Four players were tied for second while Sutton, who had won just once since qualifying for the PGA TOUR in 1981, was five strokes back at 144. In all, 67 players made the cut at five-over par 149.

Plans called for 36-holes on Sunday—a reminder of the days when both the U.S. and British Opens concluded with two rounds on the final day.

Alas, traditionalists were disappointed as heavy thunderstorms again rolled across the course Sunday morning and play was delayed just long enough to force the final round into Monday. Cook shot a consistent third-round 71 with two birdies and a bogey. It left him with a 54-hole, tournament-record 210 and a one-stroke lead over his long-time rival from California amateur days, Bobby Clampett. Sutton, with a 70, was four strokes back at 214.

Cook said the key to his success was his ability to drive the ball into the narrow and demanding fairways.

"On a scale of one to ten, I'd put driving on this course at a ten," said Cook, who missed just two fairways in the third round. "That's pretty much true everywhere, but it's especially true here."

As he was to learn, to his considerable dis-

THE PLAYERS
CHAMPIONSHIP

1983 may, on Monday afternoon. The final round saw Sutton, Cook, Clampett and Ben Crenshaw—positively ancient at age 31—hold the lead by themselves at one time or another as the lead changed hands a remarkable 11 times.

Sutton began by making birdies on three of his first four holes as strong winds whipped the course. The wind played to Sutton's advantage, because he is a low-ball hitter able to keep his shots under the wind.

After playing his way into the lead, Sutton slipped back and found himself trailing Cook and Ed Fiori after 15 holes. But on 16, Sutton made a one-foot birdie putt to regain a share of the lead.

On 17, Sutton punched an 8-iron through the strong winds. The ball ended 10 inches from the cup for the sixth and final birdie of his round. Fiori, tied for the lead, saw his chances fade when his tee shot bounced over the green and into the water.

For his part, Cook—playing in the last group—birdied 16 to get a piece of the lead and then parred 17. When Sutton parred 18 to finish with a 69 and a total of 283, Cook stood on the 18th hole knowing he needed to make a birdie to win and a par four to tie and force a playoff.

Moments later, his hopes were all but over. With water running down the entire left side of the hole, Cook hit the only shot he couldn't afford—a snap hook—and the championship was Sutton's.

"Guys like Nicklaus, Palmer and Floyd—my heroes—were in this tournament and I really felt that at least for this one time in my life I was going to beat them," Sutton said. "I may never do it again, but I got them this one time."

TOP PLAYERS OF 1983

WINNER:			
HAL SUTTON		73-71-70-69—283	$126,000.
BOB EASTWOOD	2	69-75-71-69—284	$ 75,600.
BRUCE LIETZKE	T3	68-75-71-71—285	$ 36,400.
JOHN MAHAFFEY	T3	72-74-72-67—285	$ 36,400.
JOHN COOK	T3	69-70-71-75—285	$ 36,400.
DOUG TEWELL	T6	72-74-70-70—286	$ 24,325.
VANCE HEAFNER	T6	72-71-69-74—286	$ 24,325.
CURTIS STRANGE	T8	72-75-70-70—287	$ 21,000.
ED FIORI	T8	72-73-71-71—287	$ 21,000.
DON POOLEY	T10	71-70-72-75—288	$ 17,500.
BOBBY CLAMPETT	T10	69-72-70-77—288	$ 17,500.

25th Anniversary
51

1984

It's Freddie, But Barely

Fred Couples may be the only player alive who could three-putt the final hole of THE PLAYERS Championship, edge Lee Trevino by a single stoke and still make the win look easy.

Couples "survived" the first round with a one-under par 71 that left him three strokes behind Jim Thorpe. Survived is the key word on a day when winds gusting as high as 50 miles per hour sent scores soaring and a record 64 balls into the water on the par-3 17th.

"I thought 17 was one of the easier par-5s on the course today," John Mahaffey was able to joke after his round.

For his part, Arnold Palmer wasn't that impressed by the winds.

"I'm surprised this is the strongest winds they've played in, but they're young, aren't they?" Palmer said. "I remember the 1961 British Open at Birkdale. The winds were clocked at 60 miles per hour on the first tee. All the tents were blown down and there were beer cases being blown through the air. Now that's a wind."

In the second round, Couples, who had missed the cut on the Stadium Course the previous two years, roared into a two-stroke lead with an eight-under-par, course-record 64. The 24-year old Couples, who made an eagle and eight birdies in the calm conditions, was surprised by his performance.

"I don't really like these type of courses," he said. "They're just too hard."

Oh.

Couples held the lead throughout the third round, shooting a 71 that left him two strokes ahead of Seve Ballesteros, three clear of Tom Watson and four ahead of Craig Stadler, Mark O'Meara and the 44-year old Trevino, who birdied the last three holes to shoot a 68.

"It really doesn't matter whether I play that well or not," said the semi-retired Trevino, an NBC Sports golf analyst whose practice time

1984 was limited by a bad back. "I believe that makes me a dangerous golfer. I'm just out there to waltz around the countryside and see if I can make a putt here or there."

Not many people believed that, least of all Couples who may have been young but wasn't naive.

Couples, paired in the final round with Ballesteros and Watson, struggled a bit on the front nine. He three-putted the fourth for a bogey and then scrambled to save a par from the trees on No. 6. Watson, who had birdie putts on both holes, failed to convert.

Couples righted himself, barely missing a hole-in-one on the par-3 eighth hole with a 2-iron. He tapped in for a birdie, then followed it with another birdie on the ninth hole.

"I felt quite relaxed going into the back nine," said Couples, who had won just once prior to the championship. "Every time Lee got a birdie, I seemed to get one. The eighth and ninth holes were really the crucial holes for me."

Couples came to 18 with a two-stroke lead. After safely hitting the fairway, he watched as Trevino, playing in the group ahead, missed a 30-foot birdie putt that would have cut the lead to one stroke. Couples played safely from there. He three-putted the final green, but it hardly mattered. Not only did he have the win, he also had a new tournament record, breaking Jerry Pate's 1982 total—280—by three strokes.

All that, and the PGA TOUR had a new superstar, who made a difficult game, on a perilous course, look impossibly easy.

TOP PLAYERS OF 1984

WINNER: FRED COUPLES		71-64-71-71—277	$144,000.
LEE TREVINO	2	76-66-68-68—278	$ 86,400.
SEVE BALLESTEROS	T3	70-68-70-74—282	$ 46,400.
CRAIG STADLER	T3	74-70-66-72—282	$ 46,400.
LANNY WADKINS	T5	72-66-78-67—283	$ 30,400.
MARK O'MEARA	T5	72-69-69-73—283	$ 30,400.
NICK PRICE	7	70-72-74-68—284	$ 26,800.
DAN POHL	T8	74-69-71-71—285	$ 24,000.
TOM WATSON	T8	75-67-67-76—285	$ 24,000.
JOHN MAHAFFEY	T10	69-74-69-74—286	$ 20,800.
JIM THORPE	T10	68-69-78-71—286	$ 20,800.

1985

"Calvin-ism" Is Rewarded

A 1986 biography of Calvin Peete would include a list of things he didn't do in his career: He didn't play junior golf. He didn't play college golf. He didn't even go to college. And he didn't even take up the game until he was 23.

Here's a list of things he did:

He hit a lot of fairways. He made a lot of putts. He won a lot of tournaments and he won the 1985 PLAYERS Championship, breaking the tournament record along the way.

Unlike more powerful, dramatic players, the 41-year-old Peete was simply sneaky good. Put him on a difficult course and he would shoot a few under par each round until it came down to the closing holes and suddenly he was in the thick of the fight and not making any mistakes. That was the case in 1985.

Peete opened with a two-under-par 70 that left him three strokes behind Hale Irwin, who led by one over four players. As is so often the case at THE PLAYERS Championship, the scoring reflected the weather. Both were good.

Peete kept his position in the second round, shooting a 69—139 that left him three strokes back of D.A. Weibring, at 68-68-136. A total of 75 players made the cut at two-over-par 146.

Peete made his move in the third round when he shot a second 69 to finish at 208. It could have been better, except for a double-bogey five on the treacherous 17th, when his 8-iron tee shot came up short and in the water surrounding the green. Still, Peete shared the lead with Irwin, who also shot a 69, and Weibring, whose round was typical of what can happen at the Stadium Course at the Tournament Players Club at Sawgrass. After making an eagle and three birdies on the front nine to take a four-stroke lead, Weibring made four bogeys on the back for a 72.

Peete, the winner of the 1984 Byron Nelson Award for the PGA TOUR's lowest

1985 scoring average (70.56), opened his round with birdies on the first two holes to trail Weibring by a stroke. But Weibring's lead disappeared in the wreckage of three straight bogeys, beginning on No. 5.

Peete, who missed just two fairways all day, took charge of the championship by going five-under par on the last 10 holes—a stretch that included birdies on the 12th, 13th and 14th holes.

Still, Peete knew that no lead is safe until the testy little 17th is out of the way, and once he got there, he wasn't going to spend a lot of time thinking about what could go wrong.

"I thought about 17 all night because I'd hit it in the water Saturday," Peete said after his round. "I was thirsty when I got to the tee, but I wanted to get the tee shot over with before I took a drink, so I just grabbed the 8-iron and hit it."

Good plan.

The ball wound up four-feet from the cup. When Peete made the putt, the championship was his. A few minutes later, he had a 66 for a record 14-under par 274. He also earned the praise of Weibring, who spoke for a lot of his fellow players.

"The man is a machine," Weibring said. "He drives his ball. He hits his irons and he never backed off the flag all day—and don't let anyone say he can't putt."

If they had said it before, they never said it again. Not after the show Peete put on at the 1985 PLAYERS Championship.

TOP PLAYERS OF 1985			
WINNER:			
CALVIN PEETE		70-69-69-66—274	$162,000.
D.A. WEIBRING	2	68-68-72-69—277	$ 97,200.
LARRY RINKER	3	68-72-71-70—281	$ 61,200.
GARY HALLBERG	4	72-71-67-72—282	$ 43,200.
HALE IRWIN	T5	67-72-69-75—283	$ 34,200.
DAN HALLDORSON	T5	70-68-72-73—283	$ 34,200.
BRUCE LIETZKE	T7	71-72-70-71—284	$ 27,112.
LON HINKLE	T7	71-72-71-70—284	$ 27,112.
BERNHARD LANGER	T7	68-70-75-71—284	$ 27,112.
ISAO AOKI	T7	70-75-74-65—284	$ 27,112.

1986

The Comeback Kid

John Mahaffey has known more than his share of highs and lows during his PGA TOUR career. The lows include injuries and the slumps that come with them. The highs include a win in the 1978 PGA Championship, when he made up seven strokes on the final day, and a remarkably similar win in the 1986 PLAYERS Championship.

Mahaffey's run to THE PLAYERS title began with a first-round 69 that left him three strokes behind a group of five players. It was an historic round, in one sense, since it saw Brad Fabel and Jim Gallagher, Jr. make the first holes-in-one in tournament history.

Veteran Bob Murphy (65) and Larry Mize (68) shared the lead with a record eight-under par 134 after two rounds. At even-par 144, the cut was the lowest to date in tournament history. Mahaffey, with a 69, was five strokes behind the leaders.

While playing conditions were perfect every day, the wind did begin to finally pick up on Saturday. The conditions suited both Mize and Mahaffey beautifully, and they pulled away from the field. Mize, 27, who had won just once on TOUR, shot a 66 to take a record 54-hole total 200. His four-shot lead over Mahaffey was the largest 54-hole lead in the tournament's history.

For his part, Mahaffey put on a Saturday clinic en route to his 65. He birdied three of the first four holes then birdied three in a row beginning with No. 9.

"This is about as good a round as I've ever played," said Mahaffey, 37, who had eight previous TOUR victories.

Between Mahaffey's experience, his reputation as a skilled shotmaker, and his 65 on Saturday, the conventional wisdom was that Larry Mize's four-stroke lead might not be quite enough come Sunday afternoon.

For once, the conventional wisdom was right.

Nothing on the front nine gave any indication that Mize might lose the championship. Indeed, after Mahaffey bogeyed the short, par-4 10th, he trailed Mize by four strokes. But then, beginning on

1986

No. 11, Larry Mize's world turned upside down.

Mahaffey birdied the 15th to cut the margin to three strokes. Both players bogeyed the 14th. Mahaffey picked up a stroke when Mize hit his second shot into a bunker on 15 and made a bogey.

On 16, a sometimes reachable par-5, Mize was on the fringe in three while Mahaffey hit the green in two with a 4-wood second shot. Mize stubbed his chip, leaving the ball 10 feet short of the hole. When he missed his par putt and Mahaffey got down in two putts from 40 feet, the two players were tied.

Both players parred the dangerous par-3 17th, but it was a disappointing par—if that can ever be said on the 17th—for Mize. His 8-iron tee shot left him with a dead-straight five-footer for birdie. No luck.

And so it all came down to the 18th. Both players drove safely, then Mize missed the green with his 4-iron approach shot while Mahaffey hit it with a 6-iron. Mize chipped to within four feet, then watched as Mahaffey rolled his first putt three feet from the hole.

Needing to make his putt to force a playoff, Mize missed and then looked on helplessly as Mahaffey calmly sank his putt for par and the championship.

"We stood on the 18th green when it was all over and I told Larry I was sorry," Mahaffey said. "I've been there before. I've made up many an acceptance speech walking those back nines and never had a chance to utter a word of them."

But this time, he would.

TOP PLAYERS OF 1986

WINNER: JOHN MAHAFFEY		69-70-65-71—275	$162,000.
LARRY MIZE	2	66-68-66-76—276	$ 97,200.
TIM SIMPSON	3	72-70-66-72—280	$ 61,200.
JIM THORPE	T4	69-68-74-70—281	$ 37,200.
BRETT UPPER	T4	71-65-73-72—281	$ 37,200.
TOM KITE	T4	69-69-71-72—281	$ 37,200.
HAL SUTTON	T7	71-72-68-71—282	$ 28,050.
JOHN COOK	T7	71-73-70-68—282	$ 28,050.
JAY HAAS	T7	73-68-73-68—282	$ 28,050.
DOUG TEWELL	T10	68-68-74-73—283	$ 21,600.
DAVID RUMMELLS	T10	70-65-79-69—283	$ 21,600.
BOB TWAY	T10	66-73-72-72—283	$ 21,600.
PAYNE STEWART	T10	71-67-75-67—283	$ 21,600.

1987

Sandy, Son Of Scotland

The 1987 PLAYERS Champioship had a little bit of everything. In fact, a lot of everything happened at the Tournament Players Club at Sawgrass that week in March. It all began with one of the most bizarre opening rounds in tournament history. For starters, it was plagued with thunderstorms that finally halted with fully half the field still on the course. Greg Norman led by one stroke over 10 players with a five-under par 67.

But to capture the full weirdness of the round, you only have to follow the travails of Raymond Floyd and Seve Ballesteros. The two, grouped with Andy North, began their round on the 10th hole and their problems started early. On 11, Floyd hit a decent drive, then looked on in disbelief as the ball rolled into his golf bag lying just to the right of the fairway.

Two-stroke penalty.

"It's very rare to make a bag-in-one on a par-4," said Ballesteros. "Even rarer than a hole-in-one."

After finishing the fifth hole—their 14th—play was delayed by the weather. As they waited for play to resume, Floyd and Ballesteros both hit balls into the nearby woods, trying to stay loose.

Two-stroke penalties each—and to make matters worse, Floyd hit his drive into a pond for another penalty stroke. In all, he made a quadruple bogey eight. Without the day's five penalty strokes, he would have ended the round two strokes behind Norman.

When the first round officially ended Friday morning, Steve Jones led with a 66. The second round was the same old story. Again, half the field was unable to complete play. When they did, Jones and Mark O'Meara were tied at a record 11-under par 133, five strokes ahead of Scotland's Sandy Lyle. The soft conditions resulted in the cut coming at a record low one-under-par-143.

O'Meara and Scott Simpson led after three rounds at 202, two strokes ahead of Lyle and Ben Crenshaw, but with 10 players at 10-under or better, the last round promised to be a wild one.

Neither O'Meara or Simpson could hold

1987 onto the lead, however, turning in respective rounds of 73 and 74, respectively. Both failed to birdie the 18th, which would have gotten them into a playoff. Norman made a run, tying for the lead after the 13th, but when he bogeyed 14 and parred the reachable par-5 16th, his bid floundered.

Lyle and Jeff Sluman dueled throughout their final round. On 15, both made birdies to tie Simpson for the lead, then forced a playoff with a pair of birdies on the home hole.

The weirdness continued in the playoff.

Both players parred the 16th—the first playoff hole. On 17, it looked as though Sluman might have a chance to win. Lyle's lag putt from 40 feet was close enough for a certain par, which left Sluman a six-footer for birdie and the win.

Sluman carefully studied his putt. The huge gallery around the island green was eerily quiet. But just as he was about to begin his stroke, a spectator jumped into the lake. Sluman backed away from the ball. He waited while the man was pulled from the water and taken away by security officials, then re-addressed his ball. He missed, and settled for a par.

"I might have made the putt, but we'll never know," Sluman said later.

Both players hit their approach shots to the back fringe on the next hole, the par-4 18th. Lyle chipped first, running the ball seven feet past the hole. Sluman's chip came up 12-feet short and he putted first, missing. When Lyle made his par, THE PLAYERS Championship had its first foreign champion.

TOP PLAYERS OF 1987

WINNER:

SANDY LYLE		**67-71-66-70—274**	**$180,000.**
WON PLAYOFF WITH PAR ON THIRD EXTRA HOLE			
JEFF SLUMAN	2	70-66-69-69—274	$108,500.
MARK O'MEARA	3	68-65-69-73—275	$ 68,000.
SCOTT SIMPSON	T4	69-65-68-74—276	$ 44,000.
GREG NORMAN	T4	67-68-71-70—276	$ 44,000.
PAUL AZINGER	6	68-70-68-71—277	$ 36,000.
DAN POHL	T7	68-66-75-69—278	$ 32,250.
BILL GLASSON	T7	69-69-68-72—278	$ 32,250.
TOM PURTZER	T9	69-67-72-71—279	$ 27,000.
TOM KITE	T9	72-70-67-70—279	$ 27,000.
BEN CRENSHAW	T9	70-68-66-75—279	$ 27,000.

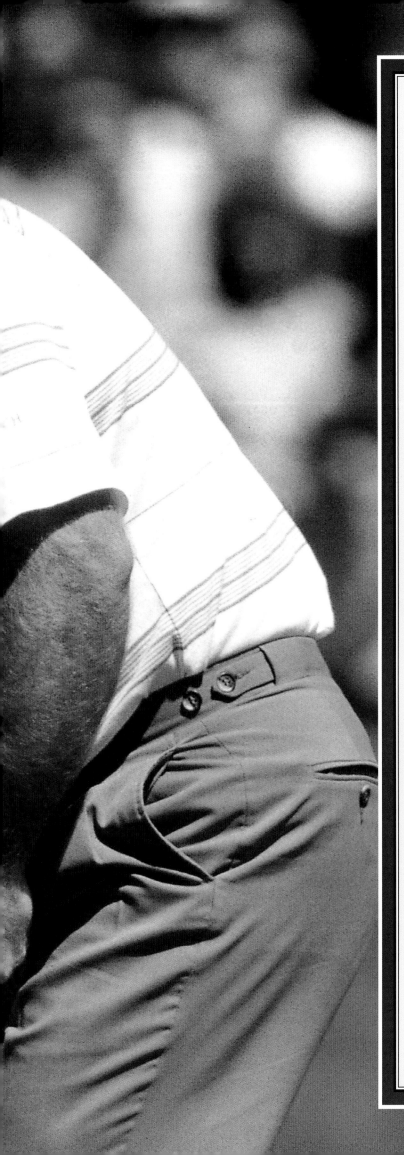

1988

A Hometown Guy Makes Good

Over the years, many of the TOUR's most popular players have won THE PLAYERS Championship, but none of their victories was more popular among the galleries than Mark McCumber's win in 1988.

For McCumber, who graduated from Jacksonville's Lee High School and pulled weeds at a local golf course to pay his green fees, his victory highlighted a career that has been a study in perseverance. It took him six trips through the TOUR's Qualifying Tournament before he got his card, but once he did, he showed he had what it takes to succeed, winning five times in the nine years leading up to his PLAYERS Championship victory.

McCumber took the first-round lead in dramatic fashion, shooting a 7-under-par 65 that included holing a 123-yard wedge shot on the ninth hole for an eagle-3. Greg Norman and Curt Byrum shot 66s to trail McCumber by a stroke going into the second round.

Playing in the morning on Friday, Payne Stewart hit 17 greens in regulation and shot a 66. That was good enough to give him the lead as McCumber shot a 72, leaving him tied with Mike Reid for second place, a stroke back.

Not nearly so fortunate was defending champion Sandy Lyle, who missed the cut, along with Larry Mize, Scott Simpson, Nick Faldo and Larry Nelson, the reigning champions of the four major championships.

The weather turned ugly on Saturday, as thunderstorms forced two suspensions of play before it was finally stopped for the day at 4:45. In all, fewer than half the field finished play. The rest had to complete their rounds Sunday morning.

The weather certainly hurt Dan Pohl, who had birdied four of his first five holes to take the lead. By the time he'd finished his third round by hitting a ball in the lake on 18 and making a double-bogey, Pohl could be forgiven if he had a grudge against the Weather Gods. He found himself four strokes behind McCumber, whose 67 put him in at 204, two strokes ahead of David Frost. Pohl would

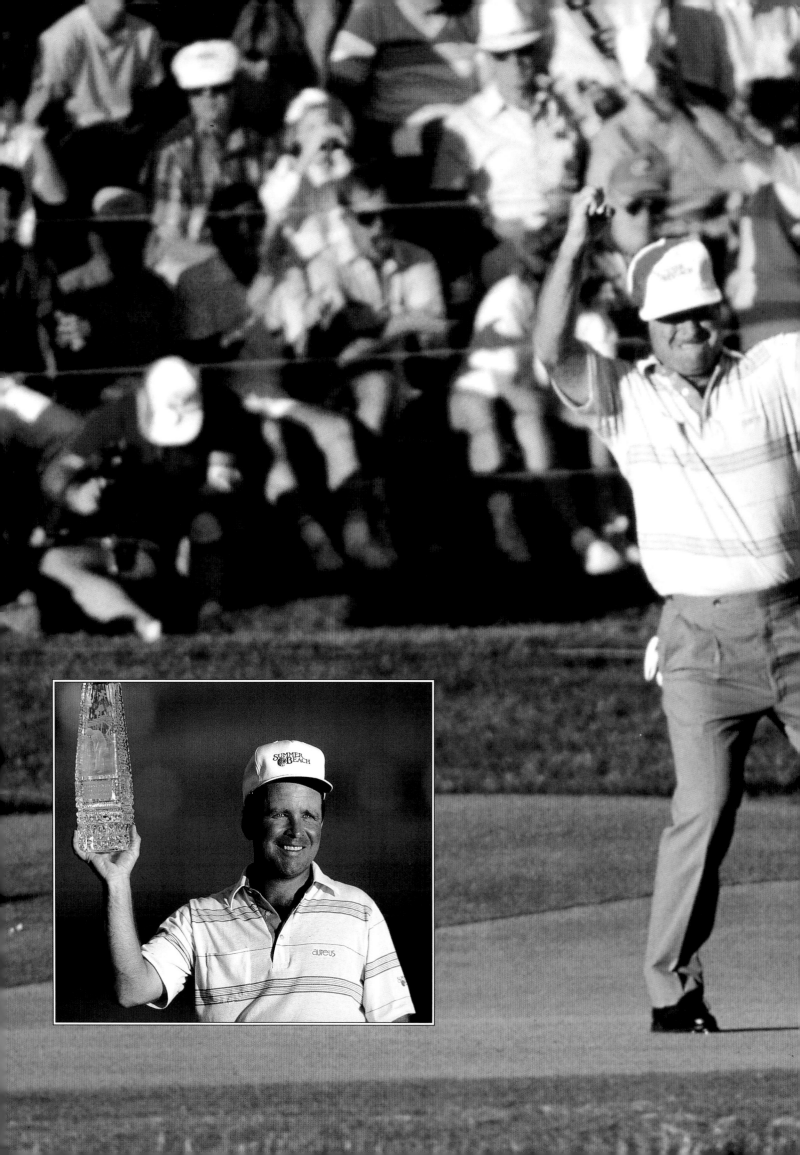

1988

finish in a tie for eighth place.

In the final round, McCumber and Frost dueled throughout the front nine, but McCumber began to pull away when he again birdied the 582-yard, par-5 ninth hole. When Frost bogeyed, it stretched McCumber's lead to two strokes. McCumber had owned the hole all week, playing it five-under par.

McCumber all but locked up his win a few holes later. He birdied the 11th and 12th holes, then watched as Frost, pressing to catch him, gambled and bogeyed the 13th and 14th.

All McCumber had to do now was avoid any of the potential disasters lurking on the closing four holes—that and keep his emotions in check. The former proved easier than the latter, which isn't surprising since any time he looked in his gallery he was likely to see his wife, two kids, parents, brothers, nieces, nephews or even his grandmother who, even though an "eightysomething," turned out for the great event.

"I can't tell you the thrills I had coming up the last three holes, seeing people I hadn't seen since grade school, seeing my family, even seeing my grandmother," McCumber said. "It seemed like I knew half the people out there."

As he walked up the 18th fairway to the enormous roar of the huge gallery, he spotted a sign that read "Jacksonville's Winner" and broke into tears. That he finished with a bogey hardly mattered, since he won by a comfortable four strokes over Mike Reid, setting a tournament record with a 15-under par 273.

"I was having trouble keeping my eyes clear so I could make that last putt," McCumber said. "I'm just tickled to death to win at home."

And the hometown fans were tickled to death for him.

TOP PLAYERS OF 1988

WINNER:			
MARK McCUMBER		65-72-67-69—273	$225,000.
MIKE REID	2	68-69-73-67—277	$135,000.
DAVID FROST	T3	67-71-68-72—278	$ 65,000.
FULTON ALLEM	T3	73-72-65-68—278	$ 65,000.
CURT BYRUM	T3	66-73-69-70—278	$ 65,000.
LANNY WADKINS	T6	70-72-67-70—279	$ 43,437.
GIL MORGAN	T6	69-70-71-69—279	$ 43,437.
DAN POHL	T8	69-69-70-72—280	$ 36,250.
PAYNE STEWART	T8	71-65-71-73—280	$ 36,250.
WAYNE LEVI	T8	70-71-71-68—280	$ 36,250.

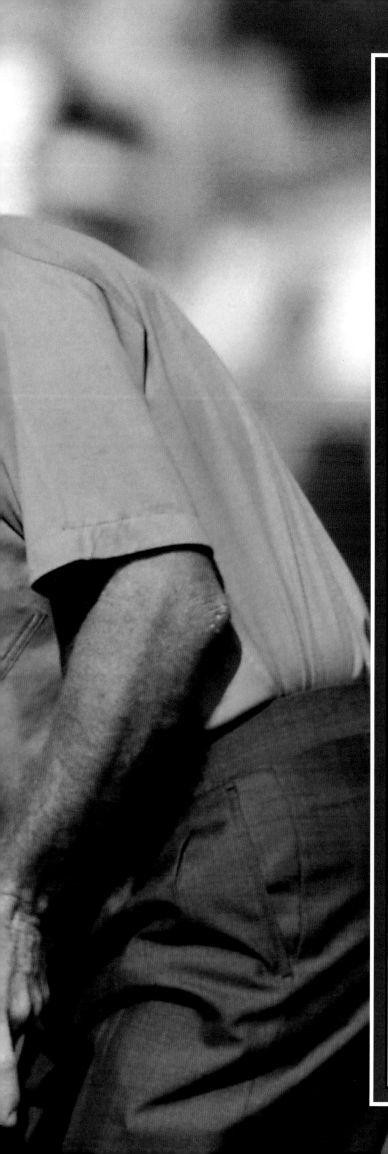

1989

Kite's Patience Pays Off

After the 1988 PLAYERS Championship, TOUR officials announced plans to refine the Stadium Course to place a greater emphasis on chipping and pitching and to make the greens putt a bit truer by switching to Bermuda grass.

No one was happier to learn of the changes than Tom Kite, widely credited with one of the strongest short games in golf. Indeed, many people believe that from 75 yards in, Kite may be the best in the game.

Not that Kite hadn't been able to handle the old set-up at the Stadium course. He held the record for both cuts made (13) and consecutive cuts (10). Still, for as much as Kite valued consistency, he valued victories a whole lot more.

Kite opened the tournament with a 69 which left him four strokes behind the leader, Keith Clearwater, who obviously was comfortable with the changes. Starting on the back nine, he birdied 11, 12 and 13 then added birdies on 16 and 17 for a record-tying 31. After making the turn, he birdied the first, third, sixth and seventh holes to get to an astonishing nine-under par with two holes to play. At that point, the course got its revenge, and Clearwater finished with back-to-back bogeys which left him with a one-stroke lead over three players.

Strong, gusty winds blew out the fog which had caused a 45-minute delay but sent scores soaring on the second day. The average score was almost two strokes over par and only 36 players bettered par 72. One victim was Clearwater, who skied to a 76 and opened the door for Bruce Lietzke, who shot a 69 to finish at 135 for a two-stroke lead over David Frost. Kite was four strokes back but still confident.

"I'm playing awfully well," he said. "Four shots is not a lot to make up on a course like this."

Kite proved it on Saturday with a 69 that left him a stroke behind Chip Beck. But the biggest—and certainly oddest—news story of the day was defending champion Mark McCumber's double-bogey five on the 17th hole. McCumber

 hit the green and barely missed his birdie putt. Then things began getting very strange. He missed his par putt and, incredibly, missed his half-inch tap-in.

The final round was vintage Kite. He was patient and tenacious, gambling only when it made sense and the odds were in his favor.

He took the lead with two birdies on the front as Beck skied to a 41 to fall five strokes behind Kite. But to Beck's credit, he fought back with three straight birdies on the back nine and closed the lead to two after Kite bogied 14.

The turning point for Kite came on the 426-yard, 15th hole. He put his approach shot into a grass bunker, hit a wedge to six feet, and made the par putt to hold his round together.

"That save was the one that kept me going," Kite said later.

That, and perhaps a bit of luck on the 16th hole.

Kite hit a perfect drive and, facing a 227-yard carry to a green guarded by water, hit what he thought was a perfect 4-wood. But the ball released and rolled ominously across the green, coming to rest just 18 inches from the water. A chip and two putts later, and he had his par.

After parring 17, he took a two-stroke lead to 18, where there would be one last bit of drama.

Kite hit a good drive and second shot, and left his approach putt two feet from the hole. Beck, grinding to the end, ran in a 25-footer for birdie, to close the gap to one stroke and cap a back-nine 32.

But Tom Kite didn't get to be Tom Kite by missing two-foot putts, and moments later he would have his second win in two weeks and his 12th victory of his career.

TOP PLAYERS OF 1989			
WINNER:			
TOM KITE		69-70-69-71—279	$243,000.
CHIP BECK	2	71-68-68-73—280	$145,800.
BRUCE LIETZKE	3	66-69-74-72—281	$ 91,800.
GREG NORMAN	T4	74-67-69-72—282	$ 59,400.
FRED COUPLES	T4	68-70-71-73—282	$ 59,400.
DR. GIL MORGAN	T6	71-69-70-73—283	$ 46,912.
MARK MCCUMBER	T6	69-70-70-74—283	$ 46,912.
ANDY BEAN	T8	68-76-69-71—284	$ 39,150.
DAVID FROST	T8	66-71-75-72—284	$ 39,150.
GARY KOCH	T8	70-69-70-75—284	$ 39,150.

1990

The Winner's Name Is Mudd

The record books list Jodie Mudd as the winner of the 1990 PLAYERS Championship but the real winner may have been the weather. It controlled the tournament months before the first drive was even hit.

A rainy fall hurt course conditions, but the real problem was an unusual Christmas gift of snow combined with a more unusual serious freeze that left the course in less-than-perfect condition.

Enter Jodie Mudd, a 29-year old, two-time winner of the U.S. Amateur Public Links Championship. Mudd believed that his experience playing public courses in less than ideal condition gave him edge and set out to prove it.

In the first round, Mudd fired a 31 on the back nine for a 67 that placed him in a tie for the lead with Mark Calcavecchia, who had finished second in his previous two tournaments. The winds picked up in the second round, making conditions even more demanding, and Hale Irwin gutted out a 68 to take a one-stroke lead over Mudd, who shot 72, and Rocco Mediate, whose 67 tied him for low round of the day.

The weather reared its ugly head again in Saturday's third round, as heavy rains pounded the course in the afternoon, causing a suspension of play with 48 golfers still on the course. When play resumed the next morning, Mudd had the lead, but it was reduced to a mere stroke when his tee shot on the island green 17th bounded over the green and into the water, leading to a double-bogey. The delay also took its toll on another contender, Tom Watson. He hit it into the water on both 16 and 17, making a pair of crazy 8s.

The final round soon came down to a duel between Mudd and Calcavecchia, and as he had all week, Mudd relied heavily on his putter. He averaged 27.5 putts for the week and used just 26 putts in the last round.

Mudd struck first, making a birdie on the

1990 par-5 second hole, the same hole he'd eagled a round earlier. He followed that with another birdie on the third hole and sank back-to-back 15-footers to save pars on the sixth and seventh holes.

For his part, Calcavecchia waited until the back nine to make his move, he birdied three of his first seven holes while Mudd birdied 14. As they stood on the 17th tee, Mudd had a one-stroke lead, and Calcavecchia had the confidence of a man just coming off a birdie.

Calcavecchia hit first, putting his ball safely on the green. He looked at Mudd and smiled. An admittedly nervous Mudd stepped up and put his ball 10 feet from the hole.

"I looked at him and said, `Tell me you pushed that,'" Calcavecchia said. "I mean, he's good, but he ain't that good."

"I kind of pushed it a little bit," Mudd replied.

Mudd knocked in his birdie putt to take a two-stroke lead with just one hole to play, but it's a hole with water running down its entire left side. Mudd played away from the lake, hitting his drive into the right rough, where it was blocked by a small tree. Calcavecchia laced a long drive down the left side, leaving him just a 9-iron approach, which ended up 20 feet below the hole. Mudd cut a 5-iron around the tree, leaving the ball just short of the green.

Now it all came down to nerves and a good short game. Mudd hit first, leaving his chip 15-feet short. Calcavecchia missed his birdie putt, and when Mudd safely two-putted he had a one-stroke victory and the biggest victory of his career.

TOP PLAYERS OF 1990

WINNER:			
JODIE MUDD		67-72-70-69—278	$270,000.
MARK CALCAVECCHIA	2	67-75-68-69—279	$162,000.
STEVE JONES	T3	75-71-69-69—284	$ 87,000.
TOM PURTZER	T3	71-73-69-71—284	$ 87,000.
BILLY RAY BROWN	T5	73-72-69-71—285	$ 52,687.
TOM KITE	T5	72-70-70-73—285	$ 52,687.
HALE IRWIN	T5	70-68-74-73—285	$ 52,687.
KEN GREEN	T5	71-69-70-75—285	$ 52,687.
MARK MCCUMBER	T9	73-72-73-68—286	$ 42,000.
ANDY BEAN	T9	73-68-72-73—286	$ 42,000.

1991

A New Wonder From Down Under

Sports-mad Australia has produced more than its share of world-class golf champions, including Peter Thomson, David Graham, Greg Norman, Bruce Devlin, Bruce Crampton, Ian Baker-Finch and Wayne Grady, to name a few.

But in 1991, there was a new name to add to the list: the winner of THE PLAYERS Championship, Steve Elkington. His victory proved that, not only had he arrived, but that he had a game that was designed to keep him around for a very long time.

Elkington beat a field that included 19 of the 20 top-ranked players in the world, and the scoring in the first round, under tranquil conditions, reflected the strength of the field. A 65 like the one shot by Bob Tway would get you the lead. An even-par 72 would earn you a tie for 80th. Elkington's 66 left him tied for second place, a stroke ahead of Paul Azinger and two strokes clear of Tom Watson.

But what a difference a day makes. On Friday strong, gusty winds blew into town and drove the scoring through the roof. Just 28 players managed to break par, led by Azinger who birdied the last four holes to shoot a 68 to lead Elkington, Fuzzy Zoeller and Baker-Finch by a stroke.

After Saturday's round, it looked as though the tournament had come down to a shoot-out between Zoeller and Azinger, who both shot 69s. Elkington shot an even-par 72 and teed off on Sunday four strokes behind the leaders.

But golf is a fickle game, and nowhere is it more fickle than at the Stadium Course.

Maybe Zoeller and Azinger had gotten into a match-play mindset. Or maybe it was just a case of putts that wouldn't fall. Either way, they opened the door and Elkington walked into contention.

The Australian made back-to-back birdies at the 10th and 11th holes, then got a piece of the lead with another birdie on the 15th. Phil Blackmar also made a move with birdies on the 15th and 16th holes, but ended his chances with a ball in the water on 18.

THE PLAYERS
CHAMPIONSHIP

1991

Elkington's chances, which looked so bright as he stood on the 16th tee, looked considerably dimmer two holes later. He missed a short birdie putt on the par-5 16th, then after hitting the green safely on 17, took three putts from 50-feet away for a bogey.

As he stood on the 18th tee, Elkington knew that he desperately needed a birdie. His drive landed safely in the fairway. That was the good news. The bad news was that it came to rest atop a sand-filled divot some 200 yards from the green.

Elkington, whose swing is one of the most admired on TOUR, calmly pulled a 3-iron and hit a draw toward the green, where the ball came to rest 12 feet from the hole. His putt hit the center of the hole and dropped in for a birdie and a one-stroke lead over Zoeller, who had one hole left to play.

Zoeller, a former Masters and U.S. Open champion, hit a perfect drive and followed it up with a 4-iron pin high and 15 feet away. Zoeller, long one of the TOUR's best pressure putters, carefully lined up his putt but slid it by the left edge of the hole.

"It fooled me," Zoeller said later. "I would have bet anything that it wouldn't go to the left. I was pleased with the way I played, but I'm disappointed. I wanted my name on that trophy. I wanted a piece of history."

The man who made the history couldn't resist a good-natured joke about life as an Australian golfer who lives in Greg Norman's shadow but finally gets a bit of the spotlight.

"Greg's the big shark and I'm just a little fish," Elkington quipped after his win. "But at least I'm a bigger fish now that I was yesterday."

TOP PLAYERS OF 1991

WINNER:			
STEVE ELKINGTON		66-70-72-68—276	$288,000.
FUZZY ZOELLER	2	68-68-69-72—277	$172,800.
JOHN COOK	T3	71-73-69-65—278	$ 83,200.
PHIL BLACKMAR	T3	67-72-69-70—278	$ 83,200.
PAUL AZINGER	T3	67-68-69-74—278	$ 83,200.
BERNHARD LANGER	T6	70-70-71-69—280	$ 53,600.
BRUCE LIETZKE	T6	71-72-68-69—280	$ 53,600.
CURTIS STRANGE	T6	71-68-70-71—280	$ 53,600.
BOBBY WADKINS	T9	68-74-69-70—281	$ 41,600.
NICK PRICE	T9	68-75-67-71—281	$ 41,600.
GENE SAUERS	T9	68-74-68-71—281	$ 41,600.
BOB LOHR	T9	68-71-68-74—281	$ 41,600.

1992

A Love-ly Victory, Indeed

For a player with tremendous power, Davis Love III goes about his business in his own quiet way. But his fellow players know that beneath his calm exterior is a true competitor—particularly when he gets near the lead. He proved that in a big way at the 1992 PLAYERS Championship.

The scoring on the first day was torrid, and while Love opened with a five-under par 67, he found himself four strokes behind Billy Ray Brown. Love made a nice move on Friday, shooting a 68 that brought him to within a stroke of co-leaders Brown and Spain's Jose Maria Olazabal.

Saturday's third round was one of those "Good news, bad news" affairs for Love. The good news was that he shot his third sub-par round. The bad news was that it was only one stroke under par and it dropped him back three strokes out of the lead. Even worse was the news that the leader was the very formidable Nick Faldo, who already had won four major championships, and who is usually a very tough player to catch.

Usually, but not always.

Faldo, known as a rock-steady putter, was betrayed on the greens, and it showed as he bogeyed two of his first ten holes and failed to convert any chances for birdies. Phil Blackmar, who started the final round a stroke back, had a roller-coaster round. He eagled the par-5 second hole to seize the lead, only to double-bogey the fifth hole followed by bogies on both the seventh and eighth holes. In all, the two men opened the door for Love, and he happily took advantage.

Very often a player can point to one moment, or one hole, that turns out to be the turning point in his round. For Davis Love III, that moment came on the eighth hole, a brutally difficult, 200-yard par-3 that might well be the most underrated hole on the course.

The eighth is a hole that has traditionally bedeviled Love, and on this day it would be more of the same. He left his 4-iron tee shot pin high but off to the right of the green, where the ball nestled down behind a mound. Under the best of circumstances it was a dicey shot, but the pressure of trailing Faldo by two strokes in the final round of THE PLAYERS Championship

1992 made it almost impossible to get close. Love knew that three would be a very good score. So did some betting types standing in the gallery.

"I heard these guys betting with each other about my chances of making a par and I didn't like the odds they were giving me," Love recalled. "I have to admit I got a little mad and decided I was going to try and pitch it in."

When he did just that, he turned and glared at the two men.

"I hope all of you lost," he told them.

The birdie got Love into the lead and, after making good putts on the 10th and 12th holes, Love had built a two-stroke cushion. But the tournament was far from over.

Love three-putted 13 and then made a world-class save from over the green on 14. His pitch from a poor lie carried over a bunker and came to rest a foot from the hole. If the birdie on the eighth hole was huge, the save on 14 was only one size smaller.

On the reachable par-5 16th hole, Love ripped a 3-iron to the fringe of the green, then nearly chipped in. One birdie down, two holes left to play.

Love picked up another birdie on 17 when his 9-iron came to within five feet of the dangerous, back-right pin. Moments later, when both Faldo and Blackmar put their second shots into the water on 16, Love knew all he had to do was keep dry on 18.

Love played it smart—and safe. He hit a 1-iron off the tee and then a 4-iron approach to within 10 feet. Two putts later and he had his fourth Tour victory.

Just how good was Love's last round?

Of the eight contenders, Love's 67 made him the only player to break par. The rest were a total of 10-over for the day.

All in all, it was a Love-ly victory.

TOP PLAYERS OF 1992

WINNER:			
DAVIS LOVE III		67-68-71-67—273	$324,000.
TOM WATSON	T2	68-70-70-69—277	$118,800.
IAN BAKER-FINCH	T2	70-67-68-72—277	$118,800.
NICK FALDO	T2	68-68-67-74—277	$118,800.
PHIL BLACKMAR	T2	67-69-68-73—277	$118,800.
TOM SIECKMANN	T6	71-72-67-68—278	$ 62,550.
CRAIG PARRY	T6	67-68-73-70—278	$ 62,550.
NICK PRICE	8	71-67-69-72—279	$ 55,800.
MARK O'MEARA	T9	69-69-74-68—280	$ 46,800.
JOHN MAHAFFEY	T9	71-71-69-69—280	$ 46,800.
JOSE MARIA OLAZABAL	T9	69-65-75-71—280	$ 46,800.
MARK BROOKS	T9	67-70-70-68—280	$ 46,800.

1993

The Price Is Right

South Africa's Nick Price came to the 1993 PLAYERS Championship as the hottest player on TOUR. Beginning with his victory in the 1992 PGA Championship, he had won five times in eight months and had 13 top-10 finishes in his last 18 events. Adding to his confidence was the knowledge that the TPC at Sawgrass played directly to the strengths of his game—accurate driving and flawless iron play.

When Price and the rest of the 146-player field arrived for Thursday's first round, they found a course that was there for the taking.

"There's no wind and there's no fire in the greens," Price said after his round. "You can throw the ball right at the pins, and it sticks."

It showed in the scoring.

Price and Kirk Triplett led the way with 8-under-par 64s that tied the first round scoring record and were just one off Fred Couples's course record on the par-72 layout. In all, 110 players finished at par or better.

While tournament officials came up with tougher hole placements in the second round, the assault continued. Price, playing conservatively, shot a 68 for a 36-hole tournament record 132 and a two-stroke lead over three players. Even a one-hour lightning delay didn't seem to hurt scoring.

"If the weather and conditions stay like this you're going to have to shoot 20 or 22 under par to win," said Greg Norman.

The winds finally blew in on Saturday, but Payne Stewart went out early and signaled the field that there was plenty of scoring to be done. Eight back at the start of the day, he hit every fairway and 15 greens to post a 66 and close to within three strokes. Price, with a two-stroke lead, birdied the fourth and eighth holes to get to 14-under extending his lead by three, but wound up shooting a 71 that left him just one ahead of Norman, Bernhard Langer and Mark O'Meara.

"It's going to be a great finish," Price said Saturday night. "They'll be some real fireworks."

Price may not have won the tournament on the 384-yard, par-4 fourth hole but he certainly

THE PLAYERS CHAMPIONSHIP

1993

kept his chances alive with what he called "the greatest shot of my life." After driving into the face of a waste bunker, he faced a steep, uphill lie from thick rough. Price hit a sand wedge to within two feet and saved a crucial par.

O'Meara closed to within a stroke of Price with a birdie on eight, but Price came back with birdies on nine, 11 and 12 to restore his comfortable lead— as comfortable as a lead can be when you know you still have to deal with the island green on 17.

The hole on 17 was cut in it's traditional Sunday placement, in the back righthand side of the green. To make matters worse, the wind was blowing from left to right.

How treacherous was it?

In all, 16 players hit balls into the water on Sunday. Greg Norman, three strokes back, decided to attack the pin and paid the price. His ball landed on the fringe, but trickled into the water. Rocco Mediate chose an 8-iron, which should have been plenty of club on the 130-yard hole. It wasn't.

"No matter how big a lead you have, that green just keeps shrinking as you get to the tee," Price remembered. "I said to (his caddie) Squeak, 'Please tell me it's a 9-iron. That's the only club I want to hit."

Price hit his 9-iron to the middle of the green and walked away with his par. He finished with a par on 18 for a total of 270 and a five-stroke victory over Bernhard Langer. Later, he was asked why he hit his shot so quickly on 17.

"I didn't want to give myself time to think about it," he laughed.

In the end, what he did think about was how remarkably well he performed that week.

"It was the best four rounds I ever played," he said. "I just hit the ball perfectly all week."

TOP PLAYERS OF 1993

WINNER: NICK PRICE		64-68-71-67—270	$450,000.
BERNHARD LANGER	2	65-69-70-71—275	$270,000.
GIL MORGAN	T3	68-71-72-65—276	$145,000.
GREG NORMAN	T3	66-70-68-72—276	$145,000.
MARK O'MEARA	5	67-71-66-73—277	$100,000.
PAUL AZINGER	T6	68-69-68-73—278	$ 80,937.
KEN GREEN	T6	70-67-69-72—278	$ 80,937.
ROCCO MEDIATE	T6	68-71-68-71—278	$ 80,937.
JOE OZAKI	T6	72-68-68-70—278	$ 80,937.
TOM WATSON	10	70-72-69-68—279	$ 67,500.

1994

The Norman Conquest

Y ears from now, when golf historians look back on Greg Norman's remarkable career, they'll point to his ability to rise to the occasion and totally dominate a tournament. Exhibit "A" might very well be the 1994 PLAYERS Championship. It was Norman at his best—which is very good, indeed.

Norman tied the tournament course record with an opening-round 63 then followed it up with three consecutive 67s. His 24-under par total of 264 beat the score of by any previous winner by an astonishing six strokes. It also put him within three strokes of the Tour's all-time tournament record, 27-under par, shot by Mike Souchak at Brackenridge Park Golf Course in San Antonio in the 1955 Texas Open.

With all due respect to Souchak's historic performance under less-than-manicured conditions, Brackenridge Park will never be confused with the Stadium Course at the Tournament Players Club at Sawgrass.

Norman lived up to his reputation by hitting 49 of 56 fairways. That, combined with fine iron play and a sublime short game, resulted in Norman going 66 holes without making a bogey. In fact, he made just one bogey in four days. No player had gone an entire tournament without making a bogey since Lee Trevino won the 1974 New Orleans Open.

Not surprisingly, Norman's first-round 63 came under ideal conditions. The greens were soft and receptive, allowing players to fire at otherwise-dangerous pins with impunity. Just as important, the winds that usually blow across north Florida in March were nowhere to be found. In all, 38 players shot under 70 on Thursday, including 1989 champion Tom Kite, who was in second place just two strokes back.

"We caught this course on a pussycat day," said former U.S. Open and Masters Champion Fuzzy Zoeller. "Just wait until the wind starts blowing."

Well, the wind took it's sweet time arriving, and Norman took advantage of the benign conditions. He stretched his lead to three after the second round and had a comfortable four-stroke lead

1994

as he teed off on Sunday, paired with Zoeller, who many felt was the only player who had a real-istic chance to catch the charismatic Australian.

If that was true, his chance disappeared very early in the round when Norman birdied the opening hole and Zoeller made a bogey, giving Norman a six-stroke lead. Anyone who thought Norman would sit back and try to protect his lead would have to think again. He birdied two of the next three holes.

It was time to start putting his name on the crystal.

Norman did finally make a bogey—not that it really mattered much at that point—on the 14th hole when a leaf tumbled across his line just as he hit his putt.

"Did he really just make a bogey?" an astonished Zoeller asked, thinking he might be hallucinating. Who could blame him?

Norman capped his victory stroll with a birdie after hitting it to within two feet of the hole on 17. Even the nastiest little par-3 in golf couldn't beat Norman this week.

For Zoeller, the man who came closest to challenging Norman, there was at least some small comfort in the knowledge that he, too, had turned in a remarkable performance. His 20-under-par 268 would have won any of the previous 20 PLAYERS Championships—many of them by a comfortable margin.

After the tournament, Zoeller put Norman's awesome victory in perfect context when a writer asked him if this had been "the best you ever played without winning?"

"Son," Zoeller said, "That's the best I've ever played and had absolutely no chance of winning."

As is so often the case when Greg Norman is at the top of his game, a lot of players knew just how Zoeller felt.

TOP PLAYERS OF 1994

WINNER: GREG NORMAN		63-67-67-67—264	$450,000.
FUZZY ZOELLER	2	66-67-68-67—268	$270,000.
JEFF MAGGERT	3	65-69-69-68—271	$170,000.
HALE IRWIN	4	67-70-70-69—276	$120,000.
NICK FALDO	5	67-69-68-73—277	$100,000.
BRAD FAXON	T6	68-68-70-72—278	$ 83,750.
DAVIS LOVE III	T6	68-66-70-74—278	$ 83,750.
STEVE LOWERY	T6	68-74-69-67—278	$ 83,750.
GARY HALLBERG	T9	68-69-69-73—279	$ 65,000.
NOLAN HENKE	T9	73-69-69-68—279	$ 65,000.
TOM KITE	T9	65-71-70-73—279	$ 65,000.
COLIN MONTGOMERIE	T9	65-73-71-70—279	$ 65,000.

1995

The Last Man Standing

H ere's the recipe for determining a true champion. Take a difficult golf course and add fast greens and plenty of rough. Throw in strong winds. Spice the field with the game's best players and stir in the pressure that comes with a prestigious championship. Let it simmer— boiling occasionally—for four rounds and...voila!

Lee Janzen is your man.

Janzen won the 1995 PLAYERS Championship the same way he won the 1993 U.S. Open at Baltusrol—he hung tough until the end while the other contenders fell by the wayside.

The scoring in the first round reflected just how brutal the conditions truly were. West winds that gusted to 30 miles per hour sent the average score soaring to 75.4 on the par-72 Stadium Course. In all, only 20 players were able to break par. A more chilling figure was 23—as in the 23 players who failed to break 80. Corey Pavin, a genius at playing shots in the wind, led with a 66 that saw him take just 22 putts. Gene Sauers was one back, followed by Janzen, Payne Stewart, Bernhard Langer and Steve Stricker, who shot 68s.

The strong, gusting winds shifted and came from the east on Friday but it didn't help the scoring. Pavin shot a 73 to lead by one at 5-under at the close of the day. With the leading score dropping from 6-under par to 5-under, it marked the first time on TOUR all year that the second round total was lower than the best score in the first round.

Sauers shot a 72 to move into a tie with Pavin, one ahead of Langer, Stricker and Davis Love III. Janzen struggled to a 74 but, like the rest of the field, could take some inspiration from Phil Mickelson, who followed his first round 78 with a 66 that allowed him to pass 83 players. In all, 30 players were within five shots of the lead.

"The course is playing so hard that if conditions stay like this, the winning score won't be far from what it is today," said a prophetic Pavin.

The third round saw Pavin grind out a 73, leaving him tied with Langer, one ahead of

1995 Janzen and two strokes clear of Stewart. The day's most dramatic disaster belonged to Nick Price. Price came to the 17th hole at 1-under par, then put two balls in the water and took a triple-bogey six. Once again, the island green had lived up to its reputation.

That Janzen went out and won the tournament on the strength of his putting is a lovely irony. The putter he used—and the one he used in four of his five previous victories—was one he'd thrown into the water on the sixth hole here three years before. Luckily, a member of the course maintenance crew retrieved it. In all, Janzen averaged just 26 putts per round, but it was down the stretch on Sunday that he was most impressive around the greens.

After a bogey on 13, Janzen made a 25-footer to save par on 14. He made a clutch putt for a birdie on 16, but then made a world-class save on 17. His 9-iron tee shot landed in the devilish little pot bunker that guards the front of the green. Facing a difficult, 30-foot bunker shot, he rolled the ball to within a foot, before tapping in for par. Still, there would be one last bit of drama.

After a safe drive, Janzen pushed his approach to the right of the green. His third shot came to rest five feet from the hole—not exactly the putt you want with THE PLAYERS Championship on the line. Still, if Janzen was at all nervous, it didn't show. He calmly made the putt—his fourth one-putt green on the final five holes—to give him a one-stroke victory over Bernhard Langer.

"Lee was very calm all day," said Payne Stewart. "He's got a great demeanor and game for tough courses. He just never seems to get nervous."

TOP PLAYERS OF 1995

WINNER:			
LEE JANZEN		69-74-69-71—283	$540,000.
BERNHARD LANGER	2	69-71-71-73—284	$324,000.
COREY PAVIN	T3	66-73-72-74—285	$156,000.
GENE SAUERS	T3	67-72-78-68—285	$156,000.
PAYNE STEWART	T3	69-73-71-72—285	$156,000.
BRAD BRYANT	T6	72-71-72-71—286	$104,250.
DAVIS LOVE III	T6	73-67-74-72—286	$104,250.
BILLY ANDRADE	T8	74-69-73-71—287	$ 87,000.
LARRY MIZE	T8	69-77-72-69—287	$ 87,000.
JOE OZAKI	T8	74-70-72-71—287	$ 87,000.

1996

Fred Couples Strolls to Second Title

Until the final round of THE PLAYERS Championship, it looked as though the tournament might produce the TOUR's fourth first-time winner of the still-young season. Justin Leonard, who joined the TOUR in 1994, after a brilliant amateur career, took advantage of rain-softened greens to join Kenny Perry with 7-under par 65s in the first round. Leonard needed only 24 putts, including a mere 11 on the back nine.

Leonard cooled off slightly on Friday and another non-winner, 29-year-old Tommy Tolles, took the lead with a 64 that put him at 11-under par 133, two strokes ahead of Leonard, who finished with a 70.

The rains returned on Saturday but Tolles hung tough in the face of the weather and an assault by the likes of Phil Mickelson (64), South Africa's Ernie Els (65) and Scotland's Colin Montgomerie (66). Tolles shot a 69 which included a brilliant par save from the trees on the sixth hole.

With all the attention on the young players, many overlooked Fred Couples who was sitting just four strokes back.

"You might need another 63 to win tomorrow," a friend told Couples, whose 63 in 1992 established a course record.

"I hope not," Couples said. "I don't have a 63 in me."

At his best, Fred Couples makes golf look like a walk in the park, even when the park has as much potential for disaster as the TPC at Sawgrass.

The question was, how would Couples' fragile back hold up? It had been just over two years since he collapsed in pain at the Doral-Ryder Open and almost that long since his last TOUR victory. If his long-time caddie, Joe LaCava, had any doubts they were erased on the first hole of the final round.

"Either Freddie has it or he really, really has it," LaCava said after the round. "Today, from the first iron Freddie hit, I knew he really, really had it."

Couples began to close in on Tolles and

1996

Montgomerie with spectacular shotmaking on the front nine. He hit it to three feet on the fifth hole for a birdie, then made a two-footer for a 2 on the treacherous eighth hole. His front-nine 32 put him within a stroke of the lead, but it was on the perilous closing holes that he finally locked up the tournament.

Standing in the fairway on the reachable but dangerous par-5 16th, he checked the leaderboard and saw that Montgomerie had just birdied 14. He knew he had to go for the green if he was going to have any real chance of winning. His 2-iron from 220 yards out looked like it was going to come up short but it barely cleared the water and somehow kicked left, leaving him with a 25-footer. He calmly holed it for an eagle, giving him a one-stroke lead.

Facing the island green on the par-3 17th, the experience and patience that comes with 11 TOUR victories, paid off. He played a conservative tee shot and then made a 30-foot birdie putt to turn up the heat on Tolles and Montgomerie.

The heat proved to be too much.

Tolles bogeyed 15, then parred in. Montgomerie's hopes sank along with his approach shot in the water guarding the 16th green. He bogeyed two of the last three holes.

Couples' 64 gave him a four-stroke victory and made the 1984 champion the first two-time winner since the tournament moved to the TPC at Sawgrass.

"I hate to admit it, but it was a pretty easy 64," Couples said.

Somehow, with Fred Couples, it always seems that way.

TOP PLAYERS OF 1996

WINNER: FRED COUPLES		66-72-68-64—270	$630,000.
COLIN MONTGOMERIE	T2	71-69-66-68—274	$308,000.
TOMMY TOLLES	T2	69-64-69-72—274	$308,000.
DAVID DUVAL	T4	70-66-68-71—275	$137,812.
ROCCO MEDIATE	T4	74-69-66-66—275	$137,812.
KENNY PERRY	T4	65-71-70-69—275	$137,812.
FUZZY ZOELLER	T4	66-70-72-67—275	$137,812.
ERNIE ELS	T8	71-70-65-70—276	$ 94,500.
JAY HAAS	T8	68-68-69-71—276	$ 94,500.
TOM LEHMAN	T8	70-72-67-67—276	$ 94,500.
VIJAY SINGH	T8	70-68-68-70—276	$ 94,500.
GRANT WAITE	T8	68-72-68-68—276	$ 94,500.

1997

"Good On You, Elk"

Steve Elkington's 1997 victory in THE PLAYERS Championship wasn't simply a great win. It was simply one of the greatest performances in golf history. Just consider that...

He led from wire-to-wire, joining Greg Norman as the only players to do so since THE PLAYERS Championship moved to the TPC at Sawgrass in 1982.

He shot four rounds in the 60s on his way to a 16-under par 272 on a course most players believed was the most demanding they'd ever faced in this tournament. After heavy rains pummeled Ponte Vedra Beach on Tuesday, the course dried out and the combination of firm, fast greens, thick, 6-inch tall rough and steady winds left players with a renewed respect for the TOUR's home course. For while it's true that the course has matured over the years, it hasn't gone soft with age.

His seven-stroke margin of victory was the largest in tournament history.

He led the field in three crucial categories: greens in regulation, putting and birdies.

All this against a field that included every one of the 50 top-ranked players in the world.

"I basically blew away the best field we've ever had," Elkington said.

No brag. Just fact.

For the stylish Australian, the win marked a return to the top echelon of the game, where he had been in 1995 when he won the PGA Championship, the Vardon Trophy and had the best record in the major championships. As the winner of THE PLAYERS Championship in 1991, it also made him one of just three multiple winners, along with Jack Nicklaus and Fred Couples.

Elkington, always respected as a pure ball-striker and elegant shotmaker, had been struggling with his putting and took a pre-tournament putting lesson from his mentor Jack Burke, Jr. Whatever the former Masters and PGA champion told his friend, it worked like a charm. Elkington opened by taking just 25 putts on the way to a 66 that gave him a one-stroke lead over

1997 a group of five players that included Major Championship winners Fuzzy Zoeller, Tom Lehman and Mark Calcavecchia.

Elkington backed up his 66 with a 69 on Friday that left just 1987 Masters Champion Larry Mize a stroke back. Slowly, steadily and most of all, patiently, the University of Houston grad was pulling away from the field.

It didn't surprise Jackie Burke.

"Steve has become an experienced player, and experienced players are the ones that can go out and make things happen," Burke said. "The other players are out there looking for answers."

Scott Hoch made his move on Saturday with a tournament-low round of 65, and when Elkington finished with back-to-back bogeys, it looked for a time as though his two-stroke lead over Hoch might be a shaky one, indeed.

As it had all week, Elkington's putting saved him on Sunday. On the opening hole, he made a tough five-footer for a crucial par. He ducked another bullet with a 15-foot par-saver on the difficult fourth hole. By the time he made a 40-footer for a birdie on eight to take a five-stroke lead, it was all but time to call in the band and strike up "Waltzing Matilda."

With Elkington cruising along with a seemingly insurmountable lead, it was left for Fred Couples to provide one grand burst of excitement with a hole-in-one of the 17th. It was only the third ace in tournament history on the famous island hole.

When, for good measure, Elkington chipped in on 18 from 35 feet away it was again time to lift a lager and toast him with the words every Aussie loves to hear:

"Good on you, mate."

TOP PLAYERS OF 1997

WINNER:			
STEVE ELKINGTON		66-69-68-69—272	$630,000.
SCOTT HOCH	2	69-71-65-74—279	$378,000.
LOREN ROBERTS	3	70-74-67-69—280	$238,000.
BRAD FAXON	4	70-69-72-70—281	$168,000.
BILLY ANDRADE	5	68-72-68-74—282	$140,000.
TOM LEHMAN	6	67-71-73-72—283	$126,000.
MARK BROOKS	T7	72-68-70-74—284	$109,083.
COLIN MONTGOMERIE	T7	70-70-71-73—284	$109,083.
TOMMY TOLLES	T7	70-67-73-74—284	$109,083.
RUSS COCHRAN	T10	67-74-72-72—285	$ 84,000.
FRED COUPLES	T10	71-74-71-69—285	$ 84,000.
ERNIE ELS	T10	68-71-72-74—285	$ 84,000.
KIRK TRIPLETT	T10	71-68-70-76—285	$ 84,000.

HOLE 1

Par 4
388 Yards

Like any good opening hole, No. 1 is challenging but takes first tee jitters into account. Most players will hit either a driver or a fairway wood from the tee, but a few long hitters will go with a 1-iron for accuracy. A drive that follows the slight dogleg down the right side of the fairway provides the best angle into the long, narrow green. That side of the fairway, however, is protected by a bunker, a lateral water hazard and grass bunkers. Trees line the left side of the hole. Players will hit short iron approaches to a green guarded on the left and front by bunkers, and pot bunkers to the right and rear.

Most players will hit either drivers or fairway woods from the tee, but a few long hitters will go with 1-irons for accuracy.

HOLE

2

Par 5
520 Yards

There are birdies to be had on this reachable par-5, but only if a player hits a good drive, preferably a high draw.

There are birdies to be had on this reachable par-5, but only if a player hits a good drive, preferably a high draw. Trees line both sides of the fairway and, in the landing area, the fairway is crowned, bringing the rough into play on both sides. A lateral water hazard and grass bunkers can come into play on the second shot. If a player does drive into good position, he faces a long-iron approach into a green that is most receptive to a fade. Players who lay up with their second shots must deal with a lateral hazard and a bunker on the right side of the hole. The green is flanked by two sand bunkers, as well as numerous mounds and grass bunkers.

HOLE
3

**Par 3
162 Yards**

Given the severity of the course's other par-3s, this is probably the easiest of the bunch—which is scant comfort for the players. Depending on the wind and the pin positions, players will hit a mid-to-short iron from the tee to the two-tiered green that slopes from back to front. The left and back-left quarters of the green are protected by a bunker, while a string of grass bunkers protects the right side. If the hole is cut to the front or middle, the players are likely to shoot right at it. However, if it's up on the second tier, many will bring the ball in low and hope it rolls back to the hole.

Given the severity of the course's other par-3s, this is probably the easiest of the bunch— which is scant comfort for the players.

HOLE 4

Par 4
380 Yards

It's a short hole, but it can be a nasty hole as well.

A classic short par-4 that demands accuracy both off the tee and into the green. The ideal drive, usually with a fairway wood or a long-iron, will be played down the right side, which is protected by a bunker and water. This offers the safest approach to the green, which is fronted by a pond that runs around to the left side of the green. If a player drives down the left side, he'll have to contend with large mounds that can block his view of the green. While an approach from the right side of the hole is preferable, it's not without its risks: that side of the green is dotted with dangerous bunkers. It's a short hole, but it can be a nasty hole as well.

HOLE 5

Par 4
454 Yards

In contrast with No. 4, this is the second longest par-4 on the course, and par is always a very welcome score. The hole sets up for a left-to-right shot from the tee, and long hitters catch a break if they can carry the plateau in the landing area. A bunker protects the right side of the hole, and players who miss it to the left may find their ball resting in thick grass on a steep, sidehill slope. The slightly downhill approach, often into the wind, calls for a long iron to a green guarded by sand and grass bunkers, as well as trees.

In contrast with No.4, this is the second longest par-4 on the course and par is always a very welcome score.

THE PLAYERS CHAMPIONSHIP

HOLE

6

Par 4
381 Yards

This hole is architect Pete Dye at his best…. any birdie will be the result of two very precise shots—and a good putt.

Trees down the right side and a bunker protecting the left side of the landing area tempt players to leave their driver in the bag on this short par-4. But this hole is architect Pete Dye at his best. The slightly-elevated, well-bunkered green is designed to accept either a wedge or a 9-iron approach but not much else. If the hole is cut to the left side of the green, the ball will feed back to the pin, giving players a good shot at a birdie. But when the pin is on the right side of the green, any birdie will be the result of two very precise shots—and a good putt.

25th Anniversary
115

HOLE 7

Par 4
439 Yards

This slight dogleg-right demands an accurate tee shot. Deep rough and trees run down the right side of the hole while a bunker and a lateral water hazard protect the left. Depending on the wind, players can face a difficult, long-iron approach. Sand protects the right side of the green but the greatest danger lies in missing the green to the left, where a deep bunker makes for difficult up-and-downs. In addition, any shot that is long runs the risk of running away down a steep slope, leaving a pitch back that is almost impossible to get close.

Depending on the wind, players can face a difficult, long-iron approach.

HOLE 8

Par 3
215 Yards

Deep bunkers and a lot of slope will test the nerves and short games of even the best players.

The longest par-3 and, in some respects, one of the most underrated holes on the course. It requires players to hit either a fairway wood or a long iron into a deep, narrow green that, while it doesn't have a great deal of slope, is generously protected. While missing it to either side is no bargain, the left side is easily the more dangerous. Deep bunkers and a lot of slope will test the nerves and short games of even the best players. All in all, this is another hole where players are very happy to walk away with a par.

HOLE 9

Par 5
582 Yards

Unlike the second hole, which tempts players to go for the green in two, this is a true three-shot hole. The landing area is generous and encourages players to take a rip from the tee. But the real story here is the second shot, usually down the right side with a long iron. Any approach shot to the left runs the risk of leaving a player blocked out by trees or stranded in a bunker. The hole narrows progressively from the tee to a green which slopes away to the right from the players. A severe bunker protects the left and rear of the green, along with a second, smaller bunker. Another small bunker sits in front of the green. Players will try to leave themselves a full wedge shot they can spin into this green. It's a hole that, when players stand on the tee, they're hoping it will make—not break—their opening nine. It's proven it can do both over the years.

The landing area is generous and encourages players to take a rip from the tee.

HOLE
10

Par 4
415 Yards

*Players will face
a mid-to-short iron into a
deceptively narrow
green.*

This hole was designed as virtually a mirror image of No. 1, so no group of players has any advantage. The drive, usually with a fairway wood, favors a draw to the right-center of the fairway, but is ultimately dictated by the hole location. The right side of the hole is protected by woods while a large bunker runs down the left side of the fairway. Players will face a mid-to-short iron into a deceptively narrow green. The green is protected by a bunker in the front right and series of grass bunkers along the left of the green.

HOLE 11

Par 5
529 Yards

Many players believe this is one of the most strategically challenging holes at the Stadium Course. A medium length par-5, if the conditions are right, players are tempted to go for the green in two, preferably from a drive down the right side of the hole. A large bunker splits the center of the fairway, along with a smaller bunker and a lateral water hazard. Players electing to lay up must choose to play to either the left or right of the large bunker. Much of the decision is based on wind conditions and pin positions. From the right side, players must hit over a water hazard and a bunker to a green which runs away from them. Playing from the left half of the fairway can offer a better angle at certain pins, but can be a slightly riskier shot.

Many players believe this is one of the most strategically challenging holes at the Stadium Course.

THE PLAYERS
CHAMPIONSHIP

HOLE

12

Par 4
353 Yards

…there are difficult pin placements, but this hole offers a good chance at a birdie.

Another classic, short Pete Dye par-4. Players can opt for anything from a driver to a long iron off the tee, but a long drive down the right side offers players a good view of the target and a pitch into the small green. There is a bunker down the right side of the hole, but the real trouble is on the left, with deep grass bunkers and huge mounds that can block a player's view of the flagstick, making even a short-iron approach difficult. The green is protected by grass and sand bunkers and there are difficult pin placements, but this hole offers a good chance at a birdie.

HOLE 13

Par 3
172 Yards

Depending on the wind and the pin position, players will hit anything from a 4- to an 8-iron to this three-tiered green. Water runs the entire left side of the hole, making the front-left pin placement the most difficult for players to attack. The front tier of the green is the highest, followed by the back-right and then the left. Besides the water, two small but deep bunkers flank the green. With the tiers and the contouring, it is not as important to hit the ball close to the hole as it is to place it on the correct level. It's an easy green to three-putt.

With the tiers and the contouring, it is not as important to hit the ball close to the hole as it is to place it on the correct level.

HOLE
14
**Par 4
455 Yards**

*The hardest par-4
on the back nine?
A lot of players think so,
and with good reason.*

The hardest par-4 on the back nine? A lot of players think so, and with good reason. Water runs down the entire left side of the hole along with a narrow bunker. Drives too far to the left may still find the fairway, but leave a player with an approach blocked by tall oaks. Towering mounds protect the right side of the hole, and there's a large bunker separating the fairway and the green. Players will be hitting mid-to-long irons into a large but undulating green. A large sand bunker protects the left side of the green while a series of smaller bunkers are strung along the right and back of the green.

HOLE
15
Par 4
440 Yards

The hole sets up for a left-to-right tee shot out of a chute of trees, but there's a large bunker that runs down the right side almost to the green that dictates caution. There is a large maintained bunker gaurding the left side of the green, but given the right hole placements, it's not quite as dangerous as it appears. There's also a smaller bunker protecting the right-front quarter of the green, as well as grass bunkers along the right and rear of the green. A large swale runs through the middle of the green and sets up the rear-right tier of the putting surface.

…given the right hole placements, it's not quite as dangerous as it appears.

HOLE 16
Par 5
497 Yards

...it's a hole that will produce problems for players coming down one of the great stretches of closing holes in golf.

This reachable par-5 requires players to draw the ball off the tee, then fade a long iron or fairway wood into a beautifully guarded green. Trees run down the left side of the landing area but even when you've driven the ball into play, the excitement has just begun. The right side of the green is protected by a pond, a bunker and a bulkhead. Players electing to bring their shots in from the left risk being blocked out by a group of trees, not to mention the thick rough. If all that weren't enough, the green is exposed to the winds and can get very firm. In all, it's a hole that will give up its share of birdies—and produce more than its share of problems for players coming down one of the great stretches of closing holes in golf.

HOLE 17

Par 3
132 Yards

Has there ever been another hole that has attracted so much notoriety so fast? The signature hole at the Stadium Course has one job and one job only: make sure that no lead is safe coming into the 72nd hole of THE PLAYERS Championship. It's a job it's designed perfectly for. Length isn't the problem. Except under the wildest conditions, players are hitting short irons into what is really a very generous green. The winds, which can swirl and gust are part of the problem. But it's really the pressure of knowing there's no bail-out, no place to play safe, that makes this hole so demanding. There's one small pot bunker protecting the front right and a ridge running through the green just to make things interesting. But at the end of the day, the rule is simple: aim for the middle of the green and pray you pulled the right club.

It's really the pressure of knowing there's no bail-out, no place to play safe, that makes this hole so demanding.

HOLE

18

Par 4
440 Yards

The green is fast and loaded with subtle breaks…a fitting hole to close out THE PLAYERS Championship.

This is a classic finishing hole. The ideal drive is down the left side, since it leaves a shorter approach shot and, generally, a better angle into the green. But water runs down that entire side of the hole, often leading players to play safely out to the right. This leaves a longer approach shot, and the right side is lined with trees and rough. The left side of the triple-tiered green is protected by a bunker which runs between the water and the bulkhead. The right side is guarded by mounds, rough and grass bunkers. Any shot missed to the right can leave a player with a testing recovery shot. The green is fast and loaded with subtle breaks. All in all, a fitting hole to close out THE PLAYERS Championship.